THE PARABLES
OF KRYON

OTHER BOOKS AND AUDIOCASSETTES FROM KRYON

by Lee Carroll

Books:
Kryon Book One: The End Times
Kryon Book Two: Don't Think Like a Human!
Kryon Book Three: Alchemy of the Human Spirit
Kryon Book Four: The Parables of Kryon
Kryon Book Five: The Journey Home
Kryon Book Six: Partnering with God
Kryon Book Seven: Letters from Home
The Indigo Children, by Lee Carroll and Jan Tober
An Indigo Celebration, by Lee Carroll and Jan Tober

Audiocassettes:
Ascension & the New Age
Changes Within You
Co-Creation in the New Age
Crystal Singer
Earth Changes
Gifts and Tools of the New Age
Honoring the Planet of Free Choice
Nine Ways to Raise the Planet's Vibration
Past Lives, Present Fears
Seven Responsibilities of the New Age

Audio Books:
The Parables of Kryon
The Journey Home

Please visit Hay House USA: **www.hayhouse.com;**
Hay House Australia: **www.hayhouse.com.au;**
Hay House UK: **www.hayhouse.co.uk;**
Hay House South Africa: **orders@psdprom.co.za**

THE PARABLES
OF KRYON

Lee Carroll

HAY HOUSE, INC.
Carlsbad, California
London • Sydney • Johannesburg
Vancouver • Hong Kong

Published and distributed in the United States by: Hay House, Inc., P.O. Box 5100, Carlsbad, CA 92018-5100 • *Phone:* (760) 431-7695 or (800) 654-5126 • *Fax:* (760) 431-6948 or (800) 650-5115 • www.hayhouse.com • *Published and distributed in Australia by:* Hay House Australia Pty. Ltd., 18/36 Ralph St., Alexandria NSW 2015 • *Phone:* 612-9669-4299 • *Fax:* 612-9669-4144 • www.hayhouse.com.au • *Published and distributed in the United Kingdom by:* Hay House UK, Ltd. • Unit 62, Canalot Studios • 222 Kensal Rd., London W10 5BN • *Phone:* 44-20-8962-1230 • *Fax:* 44-20-8962-1239 • www.hayhouse.co.uk • *Published and distributed in the Republic of South Africa by:* Hay House SA (Pty), Ltd., P.O. Box 990, Witkoppen 2068 • *Phone/Fax:* 2711-7012233 • orders@psdprom.co.za • *Distributed in Canada by:* Raincoast • 9050 Shaughnessy St., Vancouver, B.C. V6P 6E5 • *Phone:* (604) 323-7100 • *Fax:* (604) 323-2600

Edited by: Jill Kramer   Designed by: Jenny Richards

Library of Congress Cataloging-in-Publication Data

Kryon (Spirit)
     The parables of Kryon / channeled by Lee Carroll.
         p.   cm.
     Includes index.
     ISBN 1-56170-364-8 (hardcover) • 1-56170-663-9 (tradepaper)
     1. Spirit writings.   2. Parables--Miscellanea   I. Carroll, Lee.
II. Title.
BF1301.K85   1996   96-24699
133.9 ' 3--dc20   CIP

ISBN 1-56170-663-9

07 06 05 04   7 6 5 4
1st printing, August 1996
4th printing, February 2004

Printed in the United States of America

*Dedicated to the many who have read these stories
and felt the love in which they were given...
and the energy that is rich with
life-changing potential.*

Contents

Introduction

The definition of a parable is that of a simple story used to illustrate a lesson or moral. In the case of the Kryon parables, the stories are simple—sometimes even childlike—but often the real meanings are waiting for further discovery through repeated examination. Much wisdom is hiding within the facts surrounding each story, and often the shortest ones are the most powerful.

All the stories that follow were given in live sessions in front of hundreds of people who attended a Kryon seminar. Some of these stories were published in the three previous Kryon books, but many are presented here for the first time. Even the previously published ones have been altered by Kryon in order to bring them into a new understanding in this clearer energy. Don't be surprised if humor also plays a major part in some of them.

The subject of the stories, or "journeys," as Kryon sometimes calls them, is always about individual humans and how we react in specific circumstances. Kryon speaks of new gifts from God as we approach the millennium and the "new age." He speaks of good news for the future and how we have changed the planet's vibration, thus earning these new spiritual attributes. In the face of the "doom and gloom" predictions that always accompany each new millennium change, Kryon now tells us that this one is different. We have made a difference and can toss out the predictions of Armageddon and worldwide destruction. We are dearly loved by God as we have "stood in line" to be here at this time! In response to our work, Kryon is here to do his magnetic grid work, and while here, to advise and inform...and to love each of us with a compassion that comes from the creator's workshop.

Even though I am the author, the stories I have translated by Kryon have been a wonderful source of study and inspiration for me. Naturally, I have my favorites, which I will share with you as we go through them. Each story will contain an introduction and a postscript as I personally relate what it was like to translate them live and what they later meant to me.

As before, this book is created in love for humanity in this new age.

— Lee Carroll

1
Parable of the Tar Pit

———————

AUTHOR'S NOTE:

It was a chilly November day when I was invited along with my wife Jan to bring the translations of Kryon to a live session in New York at the United Nations (UN). The Society for Enlightenment and Transformation, a meditation arm of the UN, meets regularly for the enlightenment of delegates and their invited guests only. Kryon gave the shortest parable ever, and the one that summarizes how, when we change ourselves, it changes everything! This was also one of the first parables ever given in front of a group.

———————

Imagine yourself, along with many other human beings, in a tar pit covered with tar, dirty from head to foot, unable to move quickly from place to place because the tar is so thick. As you plod from place to place, you become used to this condition, and year after year your life is lived in this fashion along with the others. Like the gravity of the planet, the encumbrance of the tar is simply accepted—a fact of life for all. This is your imagined state.

Suddenly but quietly, you are offered a gift from God. It's a "magic" tool that cleans your body and keeps it clean even while you are in the tar! Like an energy field, it actually repels the tar as you walk through it. You accept the gift and the work that must go with it, and you begin to learn how to use it. Slowly you change. To others you are beginning to stand out, for you are different—fresh and clean, while they are moving around you, still in the dark tar. You begin to realize how you have co-created this for yourself, but you also realize that it was a very personal gift, so you say nothing.

Now, do you think the others around you will ignore you as you walk freely without the tar touching you or encumbering your feet? They will watch the tar touch your body and never soil you. What do you think will happen? AH! Watch! THEY are about to change! The first thing that will happen is that wherever you walk, there will be space, for they will clear the way for you. The second thing that will happen is that they will ask you how such a thing is possible. And when they find the "magic tool from God," each of them will begin using it for themselves, and more humans will also be "clean"—each person creating for him or herself personally, just as you did for yourself.

As you silently continue your life over a period of time, look at what is happening to those around you! More than half of them will be "clean" and unencumbered by the tar. Stop and think about what has really happened. You have not evangelized your gift or asked any of these people to change for you, and yet they changed anyway. This is how the result of just the one...creates for the many!

We tell you, dear ones, that when you change yourself, it is the beginning of change all around you. Humans cannot be still when they see peace and love emanating from you. It is disarming and loving all at the same time. Like a magnet among other magnets, your new polarity will eventually have an effect on the alignment of everyone around you, and your existence will never be the same.

AUTHOR'S POSTSCRIPT:

*T*ake a look at this short parable, which contains some of the clearest answers about the workings of new age energy on the planet. In this parable, Kryon has humans in a tar pit "covered with tar, dirty from head to foot, unable to move quickly from place to place because the tar is so thick."

This is how we are in normal life in the old energy, chained by old karmic lessons and walking the best we can as we carry it all around with us. Kryon then offers five words that are part of his cosmic humor. He says, "This is your imagined state." This is Kryon's way of reminding us all that the Earth experience is not reality and that our duality is a phantom. The real universe is what we experience when we are not here!

In the parable, the "magic tools from God" are the new energy gifts that Kryon speaks about. Suddenly, as you receive the gifts, the tar no longer sticks to you, and you walk around unencumbered and clean. This is a strong reference to how the new age energy affects you. You are no longer held to karmic contracts, and you can move forward on the planet toward a marriage with your higher self and eventual ascension (graduate) status. Kryon also casually mentions that we have "co-created" this magic tool.

"Wait a minute! I thought the magic tool was from God," you might say. Again, Kryon wants us to remember that he calls us "pieces of God, walking the Earth in lesson." In other words, we represent the wholeness and love of God.

Next, he has us walking around in this state without the tar touching us, indicating that not only has our old karma been dispersed, but so too the karmic ties with those who had the opportunity to interact with ours. This, of course, is the object of the parable: to show how our decisions create changes on a larger scale than just for us in our own little worlds. Kryon goes on to describe what happens to those around us. This is a really important concept, for it addresses new age energy and gifts from God.

Will we lose our mates, our kids, our jobs, and so on, if we take on the new age energy gifts? Will we be outcasts? Listen to what the parable says: "Do you think others around you will ignore you as you walk freely without the tar touching you or encumbering your feet?" The first thing is that everyone will notice that you are different, but instead of casting you out, the opposite potential exists. Others will look at how you are living and respond. Some will want the same thing and ask what happened to you, and some will just be glad that you changed. As far as mates and kids, they will see the changes in you first, and they will wonder what has taken place to make you suddenly such a great, balanced person!

When you're balanced spiritually, physically, and mentally, a wonderful thing happens: Everyone wants to be your friend! People recognize the specialness of who you are, and they are not threatened by you in any way. Can you see how this attitude would enhance a job, a marriage, a friendship, or a generation gap (and not destroy it)? The only ones you will offend are those who are angry at you for having changed—and, believe me, those are the ones you don't want around you anyway.

When it is all said and done, even though you might be the only one who decides to accept the new energy ways, dozens around you will be affected by your choice. This is part of the way God uses individual choices by humans to create energy that will benefit many. Perhaps you can see the dynamics of this concept and truly understand how an individual decision for enlightenment is far more important than it appears.

—•— —•— —•—

2
Wo and the Rooms of Lesson

———◦•◦•◦———

AUTHOR'S NOTE:

I told you that I would share my favorites with you, and this is one of them. Although this parable was one of the first ones given by Kryon, it remains strong in relevance to our daily lives. Kryon's entire thrust is to give us the tools to raise our own vibration on this planet—to be everything possible while we are here. This parable has much hidden within it that lets us actually see the possibilities we have before us. It also tugs at our hearts and asks us to "remember" who we really are.

———◦•◦•◦———

There once was a human whom we will call Wo. Wo's gender is not important to this story, but since you do not have an adequate word for a neutral-gender person, we call the human Wo—to encompass a man called Wo, or a Wo-man. However, for the sake of translation only, we will say that Wo is a "him."

Like all humans in his culture, Wo lived in a house, but Wo was really only concerned with the room that he lived in, since it was uniquely his own. His room was beautiful, and he was charged with keeping it that way, which he did.

Wo lived a good life; he was in a culture where he never wanted for food, for it was plentiful. He was also never cold, for he always had cover. As Wo grew up, he learned many things about himself. He learned which things made him feel happy, and he would find objects to hang on the wall that he could look at, which also made him happy. Wo also learned which things made him feel sad, and he learned how to hang these things on the wall when he wished to be sad. Wo also learned which things made him angry, and he found things to drag out and place on the wall that he could turn to when he chose to be angry.

As was the case with other humans, Wo had many fears. Even though he had the basics in life, he feared other humans and certain situations. He feared those humans and situations that could bring change, for he felt secure and stable with the way things were, and he had worked hard to get to that state. Wo feared the situations that seemingly had control over his stable room, and he also feared the humans who controlled these situations.

He learned about God from the other humans. They told him that being a human was a very small thing, and Wo believed it. After all, he looked around him and saw millions of humans but only one God. He was told that God was everything and that he was nothing, but that God in his infinite love would answer Wo's prayers if he prayed in earnest and had integrity during his life. So Wo, being a spiritual person, prayed to God that the humans and situations he feared would not create changes so that his room could remain the same—and God answered Wo's request.

Wo feared the past, for somehow it reminded him of unpleasant things, so he prayed to God to block these things from his memory—and God answered Wo's request. Wo also feared the future, for it contained potential for change and was dark, uncertain, and hidden from him. Wo prayed to God that the future would not bring change to his room—and God answered his request.

Wo never ventured very far into his room, for all he really needed as a human was in one corner. When his friends came to visit, this is the corner he showed to them, and he was satisfied with this arrangement.

Wo first noticed motion in the other corner when he was about 26. It frightened him severely, and he immediately prayed to God for it to go away, for it suggested that he was not alone in his room, and this was not an acceptable condition. God answered Wo's request, and the motion stopped, so Wo did not fear it anymore.

When he was 34, it returned, and again Wo asked that it be stopped, for he was very afraid. The motion stopped, but not before Wo saw something he had missed completely in the corner—another door! On the door was strange writing, and Wo feared its implications.

Wo asked religious leaders about the strange door and the motion, and they warned him not to go near it, for they said it was the door of death, and he would certainly die if his curiosity became action. They also told him that the writing on the door was evil and that he should never look upon it again. Instead, they encouraged him to participate in ritual with them and to give of his talent and earnings to the group—and by doing so, they told him he would fare well.

When Wo was 42, the motion again returned. Although Wo wasn't as afraid of it this time, he again asked for it to stop—and it did. God was good to answer so completely and quickly. Wo felt empowered by the results of his prayers.

When Wo was 50, he became ill and died, although he wasn't really aware of it when it happened. He noticed the motion again in the corner and again prayed for it to stop, but instead it became clearer and came closer. In fear, Wo arose from his bed only to discover that his Earth body remained, and he was in spirit form. As the motion came closer, Wo started to somehow recognize it. He was curious instead of frightened, and his spirit body seemed somehow natural.

Wo now saw that the motion was actually two entities who approached. The white figures, as they drew closer, gleamed as though they had a light from within. Finally, they stood before him, and Wo was astounded by their majesty—but he wasn't afraid.

One of the figures spoke to Wo and said, "Come, dear one, it's time to go." The figure's voice was filled with gentleness and familiarity. Without hesitation, Wo went with the two. He was starting to remember how familiar all this was as he looked behind him and saw his carcass seemingly asleep on the bed. He was filled with a wonderful feeling that he could not explain. One of the entities took his hand and led him directly toward the door with the strange writing on it. The door opened, and all three went through it.

Wo found himself in a long hallway with doors to rooms on each side. He thought to himself, This is indeed a far larger house than I had imagined! Wo noticed the first door with more odd writing on it. He spoke to one of the white ones. "What is in this first door on the right?" Without a word, the white figure opened the door and motioned for Wo to enter. As Wo did so, he was amazed. Stacked from floor to ceiling were riches beyond his wildest dreams! There were gold bars, pearls, and diamonds. In one corner alone, there were enough rubies and precious stones for an entire kingdom. He looked at his white, glowing companions and asked, "What is this place?"

The larger white one replied, "This is your room of abundance, had you wished to enter it. It belongs to you even now and will remain here for you in the future." Wo was startled by this information.

As they returned to the hallway, Wo asked what was in the first room to the left—another door with writing that was somehow starting to make sense. As the white one opened the door, he said to Wo, "This is your room of peace, had you wished to use it." Wo entered the room with his friends, only to be surrounded by a thick, white fog. The fog seemed to be alive, for it immediately encased his body, and Wo breathed it in. He was overwhelmed with comfort, and he knew he would never be afraid again. He felt peace where there had never been any before. He wanted to stay, but his companions motioned for him to continue, and they again started down the long hallway.

There was still another door on the left. "What is this room?" Wo asked.

"It is a place where only you can go," said the smaller white figure. Wo entered the room and was immediately filled with a gold light. He knew what this was. This was Wo's self-essence, his enlightenment, his knowledge of past and future. This was Wo's storehouse of spirit and love. Wo wept with joy, and he stood absorbing truth and understanding for a very long time. His companions did not come in; they were patient.

Finally, Wo again stepped into the hallway. He had changed. He looked at his companions and recognized them. "You are the angel guides," Wo stated matter-of-factly.

"No," said the large one, "we are YOUR angel guides." In perfect love, they continued, "We have been here since your birth for only one reason: to love you and help show you the doorway. You were afraid and asked us to retreat, and we did. We are in service to you in love, and we honor your incarnation of expression." Wo felt no reprimand in their words. He realized that they were not in judgment of him but in honor of him, and he felt their love.

Wo looked at the doors and was now able to read the writing! As he was led down the hallway, there were doors marked HEALING, CONTRACT, and another marked JOY. Wo saw even more than he had wished, for down the line there were doors with names of unborn children—and even one marked WORLD LEADER. Wo began to realize what he had missed. And, as if they knew his thoughts, the guides said, "Do not be reproachful with your spirit, for it is inappropriate and does not serve your magnificence." Wo did not fully understand. He looked back down the hallway from where he had first entered and saw the writing on the door, the writing that had originally frightened him. The writing was a name! It was HIS name, his real name...and He now fully understood.

Wo knew the routine, for now He remembered everything, and He was no longer Wo. He said good-bye to his guides and thanked them for their faithfulness. He stood for a long time, looking at them and loving them. Then He turned to walk toward the light at the end of the hallway. He had been here before. He knew what was waiting for him on his brief three-day trip to the cave of creation to retrieve his essence—and then on to the hall of honor and celebration, where those who loved him dearly were waiting for him, including those whom He had loved and lost while on Earth.

He knew where he had been, and he knew where he was going. Wo was going home.

AUTHOR'S POSTSCRIPT:

The introduction of the character, Wo, by Kryon in the early stages of storytelling is an attempt at creating a person with no gender. Wo is a wo-man—which is it, woman or man? It is Kryon's intent to avoid creating a gender slant to interfere with your full understanding of the parable or your ability to put yourself in Wo's place.

In the parable, Wo's home is obviously his life, or his "expression" (as Kryon calls a lifetime) on Earth. The analogy of the various rooms refers to the windows of opportunity that we all get, which come along with our contract, our karma, and therefore our potential while we are here.

The part about Wo learning what makes him happy, sad, and angry, and then hanging things on the wall to make him feel that way, is really insightful information about humans. It refers to the parts of ourselves that dig into the past and revisit events in order to feel a certain way. Usually, it's not appropriate, enlightened behavior, since it dredges up old memories so that we can "feel" anger, hate, vindictiveness, and victimization. Sometimes it's just good old wishing to be in a place that made us happy—such as when we were growing up.

The fact that Kryon said that Wo "placed things on the wall" for this purpose was also meaningful. When you come into my home, the items on the wall are for all to see. They are my family photos and works of beauty. What this means is that I have placed things on the wall to give them emphasis, even for the benefit of strangers who come in, because I feel that these items are special. Therefore, Kryon has Wo hanging his feelings up for everyone to see and react to on his "wall" of lesson. Wo, like so many humans, wants to involve others in his own process, since it makes him feel better to do so. Wo doesn't know about responsibility yet. Even so, later on we learn that no matter what stage

Wo is at in the enlightenment department, there is no judgment from God about it—ever.

We see that Wo has fears, and his main one is about control. It seems that in his life he fears the situations where someone could change his room (his life). His reaction to most of these fears is to stay the same. His real fear, therefore, is change, and he longs for stability, or a static awareness. He also fears the past, but he doesn't know why. He turns to other humans to learn about God, and he uses what he learns to protect himself from change. This is an excellent example of what religion is teaching today. We have God playing the role of responsible protector from evil, and church members are encouraged to follow the shepherd's protection through the valley of the shadow of death. This hardly encourages empowering spiritual thought from individuals. Nor does it promote the concept of taking responsibility for what happens to you, as Kryon has advised us we might consider.

The wonderful part of this story is that even though Wo "buys" into the average, normal kind of religious doctrine, he gets results from his prayers! He receives the protection he asks for, and he is indeed shielded from change and from the disturbing motion in the corner. Again, Kryon has told us that the mechanics of the Spirit of God are absolute and that the loving energy of good, prayerful intent yields results. Remember the adage: "Be careful what you ask for—you might get it"? It's true! And this parable is the proof.

We all get various chances for empowerment and self-discovery in every lifetime, and Wo got his. Even though he felt he had satisfactory answers, God honored him with a "poke" from his guides. This was the irritating motion he saw in the corner, along with his vision of a door. It was his guide's efforts to bring him into another reality, thereby giving him his deserved opportunity for change—and a chance to face his fear. It was again insightful of Kryon to show what the religions of the day told him to do about it: Wo was told that the motion was evil. To this day, this is the most oft-quoted answer for anything contrary to popular doctrine, no matter what the religious belief. Many who disagree with another's point of view simply call it evil and never truly address any of the messages or look at the energy that surrounds the belief.

So Wo finally died, and the thing he feared the most happened: The motion in the corner became reality. But he somehow recognized it and was not frightened. We go on to see the various rooms beyond the door, and we share in Wo's discovery.

The room tour is an exposure of his earthly contract (the one he made for himself), and along the way his potential enlightenment—with riches, peace, and personal inner essence of individual power, his "piece of God." He recognizes his guides along the way, showing us that we know who our guides really are, but we have this hidden from us while we are here. Imagine going through life with two or three friends ready to help us and love us at every step—and ignoring them! Wo did this very thing, and yet his guides did not stand in judgment of him. Such is the stuff that the love of God is made of.

Wo began to get the picture and to feel that he had fouled up terribly. The guides, however, set him straight immediately and told him, "Do not be reproachful with your spirit, for it is inappropriate and does not serve your magnificence." This was Wo's crossover. At that moment, he went from being a "past human in lesson" to becoming what he always was: a piece of God, a universal entity. The next thing he looked at was his real name on the door, and he remembered everything.

When Kryon presents journeys and parables, he actually takes me "there" during the live translation. In the case of this parable, I got to feel the wind and weather, and so forth. Kryon often lets me describe what I am "seeing," in addition to his thought groups given to me for translation. In the process, however, I am affected greatly, often weeping with the joy of full understanding of what is being presented while I sit in my chair. There is nothing that I can describe that is close to this experience in comparison, except what we get to feel in a very, very real dream.

I actually stood there as Wo did, poised at the brink of going home—bathed in love. I felt the tug of love from those who were already there, and I longed for my friends on the other side. I saw my brilliant, glowing guides and felt their love, and then I took the hand of Kryon and returned to my chair in the gathering in Del Mar, California.

3

The Big, Fuzzy Caterpillar

AUTHOR'S NOTE:

For children, apparently, this parable has a message that is unmistakable. When presented live, the doubting caterpillar has a deep, tired voice. You might even recognize the caterpillar when you read this—many do. It is also one of my favorites.

The forest was bustling with life, and underneath the low foliage canopy of the ground cover, the big, fuzzy caterpillar was speaking to his group of caterpillar followers. Not much had changed in the caterpillar community. The big, fuzzy caterpillar's job was to watch over the group so that all the old ways were kept and respected. After all, they were sacred.

"Word has it," said the big, fuzzy caterpillar between bites of his ever-present leaf meal, "that there is a spirit of the forest who is offering caterpillars everywhere some big new deal." Munch-munch. "I have decided to meet with this spirit and advise you on what we are supposed to do."

"Where will you find the spirit?" asked one of the followers.

"It will come to me," said the big, fuzzy one. "After all, can't go too far, you know. No food beyond the grove. Can't be without food." Munch-munch.

So when the big caterpillar was alone, he called out loud for the spirit of the forest, and before too long, the great, quiet spirit came to him. The forest spirit was beautiful, but much was hidden since the caterpillar wasn't known to leave his cozy leaf bed.

"I can't see your face very well," said the big caterpillar.

"Come a bit higher," said the spirit of the forest in a kind voice. "I am here for you to see." But the caterpillar remained where he was. After all, it was his house, and the spirit of the forest was there by invitation.

"No, thanks," said the big, fuzzy one. "Too much trouble right now. Tell me, what's all this I hear about some big miracle that's only available to caterpillars—not ants or centipedes—just caterpillars?"

"It's true," said the spirit of the forest. "You have earned a gift that is amazing. And if you decide you want it, I will tell you how."

"How did we earn it?" asked the big, fuzzy one, busy with his third leaf since the conversation started. "I don't remember signing up for anything."

"You earned it through your wonderful lifetime efforts to keep the forest sacred," said the spirit.

"You bet!" exclaimed the caterpillar. "I do that every day, every day. I'm the leader of the group, you know. That's why you're talking to me instead of just any caterpillar." Upon hearing this comment, the forest spirit smiled at the caterpillar, although the caterpillar couldn't see it since he had decided not to get off his leaf. "I've been keeping the forest sacred now for a long time," said the caterpillar. "What do I get?"

"It's an amazing gift," replied the forest spirit. "You are now able, through your own efforts, to change into a beautiful winged creature and fly! Your colors will be amazing, and your mobility will startle all who see you. You can go anywhere you wish in the forest by flying above it. You will be able to find food everywhere and meet new, beautiful winged creatures as well. All this you may do immediately if you wish."

"Caterpillars that fly!" mused the fuzzy one. "That's unbelievable! If this is true, then show me some of these flying caterpillars. I want to see them."

"It's easy," replied the spirit. "Just travel to a high place and look around you. They are everywhere, flitting from branch to branch having a wonderful, abundant life in the sun."

"Sun!" exclaimed the caterpillar. "If you really are the forest spirit, you know that sun is hot for us caterpillars—bakes us, it does—isn't good for our hair, you know...have to stay in the dark—nothing worse than a caterpillar with bad hair."

"When you change into the winged creature, the sun enhances your beauty," said the spirit kindly and patiently. "The old methods of your existence will change dramatically, and you will leave the old caterpillar ways on the floor of the forest while you soar into the new ways of the winged ones."

The caterpillar was silent for a moment. "You want me to leave my comfortable bed here and travel to a high place in the sun to see proof?"

"If you need proof, that's what you have to do," replied the patient spirit.

"No," said the caterpillar, "can't do that—have to eat, you know. Can't go to strange high places in the sun to gawk when there's work here. Too dangerous! Anyway, if you were the forest spirit, you would know that caterpillar eyes point down, not up. The great Earth spirit gave us good eyes that point down so we can find food—any caterpillar knows that. What you ask isn't very caterpillarlike," said the increasingly suspicious fuzzy one. "Looking up isn't something we do much of." The caterpillar was silent for a moment. "So how do we accomplish this flying thing?"

The spirit of the forest then explained the process of metamorphosis. He explained how the caterpillar had to commit to the change, since he could not reverse it after it started. He explained how the caterpillar used his own biology while in the cocoon to change into a winged creature. He explained how the change would require a sacrifice, a time of quiet darkness while in the cocoon until all was ready for the graduation into a beautiful, multicolored flying creature. The caterpillar listened quietly, not interrupting except for the munching noises.

"Let me get this straight," the caterpillar finally said irreverently. "You want us all to lie down and give intent for some biological thing that we have never heard of to take us over. Then we are to let this new biological thing encase us totally in the dark for months?"

"Yes," replied the spirit of the forest, knowing only too well where the conversation was going next.

"And you, as the great forest spirit, won't do this for us? We have to do it ourselves? I thought we earned it!"

"You earned it," said the spirit quietly. "And you also earned the power to change yourselves in the new forest energy. Even as you sit on your leaf, your own body is equipped to do it all."

"What happened to the days when food fell from heaven, waters parted, and the walls of cities fell down—stuff like that? I'm not stupid, you know. I may be big and fuzzy, but I've been around awhile. The spirit of the Earth always does the big work, and all we are supposed to do is follow instructions. Anyway, if we all did what you asked, we would starve! Any caterpillar knows that you have to eat all the time..." Munch-munch. "...to stay alive. Your big new deal sounds pretty suspicious to me."

The caterpillar thought for a moment and said, "Dismissed!" to the forest spirit, as he turned around to find where the next bite was coming from. The forest spirit quietly departed as asked, as he heard the caterpillar mumbling to himself, "Caterpillars that fly! My left feet!" Munch-munch.

The next day, the caterpillar issued a proclamation and gathered his followers together for a conference. All was still as the crowd listened intently to find out what the big, fuzzy one had to say about their future.

"The spirit of the forest is evil!" proclaimed the caterpillar to his followers. "He wants to trick us into a very dark place where we will surely die. He wants us to believe that our own bodies will somehow turn us into flying caterpillars—all we have to do is stop eating for a few months!" Great laughter ensued at this remark.

"Common sense and history will show you how the great Earth spirit has always worked," continued the caterpillar. "No good spirit will ever take you to a dark place! No good spirit will ask you to do something so Godlike by yourself! These are all tricks of the great evil forest spirit." The caterpillar swelled up in self-importance, ready for the next comment. "I have met with the evil one and have recognized him!" The other caterpillars went wild with approval at this remark, and they carried the big, fuzzy one on their smaller fuzzy backs in circles while they gave him praise for saving them from a certain death.

We leave this festival of caterpillars and gently move up through the forest. As the commotion below begins to fade from our ears, we pass through the canopy of leaves that shields the bottom of the forest from sunlight. We gently move up through the darkness of the leaves into the area reserved for those who can fly. Even as the din of celebrating caterpillars is gradually lost to our ears, we experience the grandness of the winged ones. Flitting from tree to tree in the bright sunlight are multitudes of gloriously colored free-flying caterpillars called butterflies, each one decked in the splendor of rainbow colors, some that were even former friends of the big, fuzzy, dark one below—each one with a smile and plenty to eat—each one transformed by the great gift from the spirit of the Forest.

AUTHOR'S POSTSCRIPT:

Like so many other parables, this little one about a simple caterpillar has multiple messages and some insights about the way God treats us with unconditional love. It also speaks of our current Earth changes.

Kryon chose the caterpillar because we all have known since we were kids that, indeed, caterpillars go through an amazing metamorphosis and become flying multicolored butterflies. It's the classic story in nature of an ugly, fat, hairy worm with lots of feet, turning into a beautiful, peaceful flying butterfly—the former we brush off of us with disgust (and girls scream a lot), and the latter we welcome to sit on our hand or nose! The facts, therefore, are common to all, and so the story takes on a special significance.

This parable is about something that is real, but which seems to be fearful or illogical when analyzed by the standards of an intellect that worships only the old methods. If caterpillars really could think and hold meetings, I guarantee that some would never go into metamorphosis! They would also tend to polarize themselves politically into the ones that did and the ones that didn't—and typically, they would probably never look around to see what the ones that did were like. This is because it is absolute human nature to get into a groove and stay there if it even marginally works for us. Even in the darkest places there is resistance to change, since sometimes we burrow into our holes and surround ourselves with the old ways.

Through time, the old ways become sacred, and the new ways become blasphemous. The silliness of a caterpillar rejecting the change into a butterfly, unfortunately, is not unlike what humans do daily! Not satisfied to simply reject spiritual change, some humans form organizations and evangelistically tell all they meet to follow their lead. Somehow it makes them stronger to entrench themselves with others of like minds around them—especially those whom they have convinced. History is filled with tragedy after tragedy of cult leadership and death, and it continues today.

How many people do you know who have rejected something new for no reason other than what they have is "good enough"? Even when presented with gifts, some either feel unworthy to take them or feel it has to be some kind of trick. This is due to fear-based thinking and decision making that is the staple of old Earth energy. In the case of the caterpillar, he was afraid he wouldn't be able to continue his food fetish if he left his abode—even to prove that caterpillars could fly! Metaphorically, this is a way of saying that we make fear-based decisions that keep us from advancing through faith to the next level of awareness. Some of us won't even make a trip to a meeting or a store or to a friend's house to examine something that another has said is wonderful or amazing. We think to ourselves, It can't be true, therefore it isn't. Then we go on about our business and remain in the dark.

How does God treat us when we do this? This parable, along with so many others that Kryon has given, shows us the unconditional love of God. It speaks of the fact that God is here with won-

derful information and energy gifts in the new age for those who wish to envelop them. Those who do not are not judged, and best of all, those who decide not to believe are not evangelized. Notice that the spirit of the forest, even though he knew of the caterpillar's mindset, did not defend the new gifts or try to talk the caterpillar into anything. The spirit of the forest simply loved the fuzzy caterpillar no matter what the caterpillar did, and he spoke the truth to him. It was up to the caterpillar to discern if the truth belonged to his life or if he would stick to what worked at the moment. Did you notice that the spirit of the forest asked the caterpillar to DO SOMETHING in order to find the proof? The old methods don't support such a thing. In the old days, proof was always brought to us. Therefore, the caterpillar decided not to look.

If there is any sadness in this parable, it is in the fact that the caterpillar leader affected the lives of many surrounding him. He stopped their growth with a fear-based message and kept them from deciding something important for themselves. Many, therefore, would never see the sunlight, the freedom, and the colors. Many would be washed away when the rains flooded the bottom of the forest, instead of taking flight to the shelter of a dry tree.

Kryon has told us that we are sitting in the greatest spiritual change that has ever taken place, and that the Earth will resound with our new vibration. Look around you. Do you think things are changing on this planet? For example:

(1) The consciousness of peace: Today, where the ancient scriptures told us the deserts would be running red with blood by now, there are two countries negotiating water rights instead. Political prisoners who used to be incarcerated by dictatorships are now presidents of their own countries. The "evil empire" came tumbling down awhile ago. Did you notice?

(2) Elements: Seen anything different about the weather patterns? Kryon told us that our entire crop-growing scenario will

change. Seen any floods lately? Or winter conditions during spring? Or big winds at a pace unheard of in your lifetime? Or volcanoes where they were supposed to be dormant? Think about it.

(3) Earth's frequency: Did you know that the Earth's base frequency, called the Schumann resonance (SR), has for decades been at 7.8 cycles per second? The military built its entire communications systems based on an assumed constant SR. Suddenly, it has moved to 8.6 and continues to climb.

(4) Magnetics: Did you know magnetic north is on the move? Did you know that the strength of the Earth's magnetic field is lessening? What does this all mean? Kryon tells us that the Earth is responding to the fact that we are raising the vibration of the planet and that we have new gifts from God to assist us.

What do you think about those who ignore all these signs and cling to the old ways when all around them the planet is shouting, "THINGS ARE CHANGING"? The caterpillar did, and he took many with him in the process.

Munch munch . . .

4
The Missing Bridge

AUTHOR'S NOTE:

How many of us really do not trust our intuition? Or, for that matter, how many of us have difficulty with faith? Notice, please, that my own hand is raised. "Trust in things not seen" is one of the hardest principles of a belief system that has us trusting in God and ourselves for our future. This is the kind of story that Kryon often gives that is instructional within the parable. Read the story of **The Missing Bridge.**

Dear ones, the only thing that separates you from the mind of God is the duality that you have created for your incarnation here. When you reach out and trust that portion of your spirit that resides above you, you are using the new gifts of God in this new age.

Henry was on a road, traveling quickly. His journey was to the other side of the valley, and in all appropriateness, Henry, being an enlightened human, had asked God to co-create this journey with him. He knew intuitively that this had been a proper and correct thing to create for himself, and so he had indeed created it. He was on the road, but there was one very real problem: There used to be a bridge on the road to the other side of the valley, but it had been missing now for some time. Yet Henry continued down the road with full knowledge that the bridge was out. You see, Henry was in the process of creating a miracle of trust regarding his future, and he had committed himself to the process of faith.

Had Henry lost his mind? What would a normal human think at this time? The human mind makes assumptions: "The bridge is not there; therefore, I will die." "The bridge cannot be rebuilt quickly enough—it was not there last night when I passed the same point! Therefore, it's not going to be there tonight." The assumption is that the human expects the bridge to be as it was before, made by other humans with steel and concrete, in the same place as before. "My vehicle will not make it if there is no bridge," the human says.

Henry, on the other hand, was trying for the first time to co-create his future with the new gifts of God in the new age. He had learned that he was no longer a victim of his life or the circumstances around it. He had taken responsibility for everything around him—including the missing bridge—and was moving forward in a manner that would take him to places he had never been, or had been afraid to go. Henry was trusting God for the first time! He was full speed ahead and looking at an empty abyss where the bridge used to be. What did Henry know that most humans don't? Here are the admonishments for faith in this new age:

(1) Do not think like a human when it comes to things of God! Think like God would. There is much going on that you are unaware of when God co-creates with you to make large changes in your life. Things that seem utterly impossible will take many strange twists to become your reality.

(2) Make no adjustments along the way out of fear! You see, if you think like a human, you will indeed create fear first. Your intellect will work against you in this circumstance, shouting in your ear to turn left or right on your journey—speeding toward the bridge that isn't there. You may choose to stop altogether and abandon your journey due to the steel grip that fear can have on your heart.

(3) Take responsibility for the journey! Listen closely, for this is the important attribute. If you think like a human and fear like a human, you won't have trust and will blame God for what may appear to you as a negative situation. "Here I am on the road, speeding to my death! God, you have deceived me! God, you have betrayed me! I will surely be dashed into the canyon below!" Your imagination will work overtime to convince you that nothing you could ever do will make a difference—such is the

duality that you have given yourself while on Earth.

If you take responsibility for the journey, then God cannot do anything "to you." You are part of God! You are co-creating on the road, thinking as God thinks—unafraid, knowing that where the bridge once stood there will be something to replace it, without assumptions of what it might be.

As Henry sped toward the valley, suddenly he saw ahead of him just what he thought he'd see—the bridge was indeed still missing. It wasn't possible to be rebuilt by humans in a day, and he knew that. Henry was afraid. It was the last moment, and he knew that his test was at hand, but what was this that Henry also saw? There were others standing on the road waving him on around a curve to an area he had never seen before—and coming into view was a brand-new bridge—a bridge that had taken a full year to build! This was a bridge that had been under construction long before Henry had ever asked for it or needed it! It was wider than the one he expected. It had lights to show the way at night, and it moved him easily across the valley to the other side. It had been constructed completely out of sight and only revealed itself now—when he needed it the most.

Henry stopped his vehicle on the other side of the valley and held a brief ceremony. He thanked God for the power of co-creation, and God responded by thanking Henry for raising his vibration—and that of the planet—by trusting in the "reality of the unseen."

AUTHOR'S POSTSCRIPT:

*I*f you understand this parable, you will understand what God has for you in this new energy. Kryon tells us that God's time is not linear! It's in the "now," meaning that past, present, and future do not fall in the same kind of linear straight line that humans experience. God is actually building the answers before our questions! Just like the bridge, God is co-creating the solutions before we ask. This is done in all appropriateness, since our windows of opportunity were set up by us in advance of our life here. Don't confuse this with predestination. We are on the planet of free choice, but God has the advantage of knowing "in advance" what we will need in our time line IF WE HAPPEN TO ASK. The setups are in place now for what we will co-create and manifest tomorrow—for healings, for abundance, for partnerships, and for life's most difficult times. These setups are created by God to honor requests that have not even been conceived by us yet! Such are the wonderful ways of faith and what Kryon calls "co-creation with God."

Perhaps this will give you a different perspective of why trust (or faith) works at all. This parable shows us that even as Henry asked for his bridge to be there, it had been started a year earlier. Are there things in your life that look impossible to create due to circumstances that you feel are set for life—for example, a job that will "never get better," or a family circumstance that can "never change"? Do you feel stuck with lack of finances, or are you on a path that you feel is taking you nowhere? How would it make you feel to absolutely know that the answers to these impossibilities were in progress right now—and simply waiting for you to give intent to make them happen.

Take another look at the three admonishments within the parable, for even if your name isn't Henry, the story is for you. Isn't it time for you to get on with why you are here?

5

The Father and the Son

AUTHOR'S NOTE:

*Here is a story that many men will relate to. Are you the father. . .
or the son? Even if you are neither, or not even a male, this story
is relevant to our planet. It is a story about hatred—the kind that
lasts for a lifetime—one of the supreme tests of human nature.
Hatred is like a coiled spring. What most people don't know is that
when uncoiled, it has a powerful potential to be turned into love!*

Now let me tell you the story about the father and the son. Let the love saturate every pore of your body as the truth of this real story unfolds to you. Now is the time for the healing that you may have asked for earlier, for healing will come with action. Action is the result of knowledge.

And so there was on the planet Earth, the father. Now, he was not yet a father but was looking forward to it, for the birth of his child was imminent. He so hoped that the infant would be a boy, for he had great plans for a male child. The father was a carpenter, and he wished to teach the son carpentry. "Oh, I have so many things to teach him," he would say. "I will teach him the tricks of the trade, and I know he will be excited and will carry on the name of our craft within this family." And so when the birth occurred and indeed it was a boy child, the father was overwhelmed with joy. "This is my son!" he cried to everyone. "This is the one who will carry the honor of the family. This is the one who will have my name. This is the great new carpenter, for I will show him everything I know. We will have a grand time together, my son and I."

And so as the baby grew up and became older, he loved the father. For, the father doted over him, lifting him up at every opportunity, saying, "Son, just wait until I can share these things with you! You're going to love it. You will share our lineage and our craft and our family, and we will be proud of you long after I am gone." But something unusual happened along the way. As life progressed, the son slowly felt smothered by the father's attention, and he began feeling that he had his own path, even though the son did not recognize it in those words.

The son began rebelling in small ways. When he reached the teen years, he was not interested anymore in what the father had to say about carpentry or lineage.

He said respectfully to the father, "Father, please honor me; I have my own wishes and desires. There are things I'm interested in that are not carpentry."

The father could not believe what he was hearing and said, "But son, you don't understand! You see, I'm wiser than you, and I can make decisions for you. Let me show you these things. Trust me. Let me be what I was supposed to be as your teacher, and we will have a grand time, you and I."

"I don't see it that way, Father. I do not wish to be a carpenter, nor do I wish to hurt your feelings, sir. But I have my own path and wish to go my way." That was the last time the word *sir* was used, for the honor between father and son gradually disintegrated and diminished until it became a void of blackness and darkness.

As the son grew even more, he realized that the father continued to badger him to become something he did not wish to be. And so the son left home, not even saying good-bye to the father, but instead, leaving a note that said, "Please leave me alone."

The father was appalled. My son, he thought, I have spent 20 years waiting for this time. He was supposed to be everything—the carpenter, the grand master of the craft with my name. I am ashamed. He has ruined my life!

The son also thought, This man has ruined my childhood and shaped me into something I had not chosen to be. And I do not choose to have affection for him. And so there was, indeed, anger and hatred between the father and the son, and it remained all of their lives. And when the son had a child of his own, a beautiful daughter, the son thought, Perhaps, just perhaps, I should invite my father to see this child of his lineage. But then he reconsidered, thinking, No, this is the father who ruined my childhood and hates me. I am not going to share anything with him. And so the father never got to see the grandchild.

And so it goes that in his 83rd year, the father died. And on his deathbed he looked back and he said, "Perhaps now, as my death is near, I will call for my son." And so in his moment of wisdom, feeling death closing in, he sent for the son.

The answer came back from the son, saying, "I don't care about you, for you ruined my life. Stay away from me." And then the son added, "I will be glad of your passing!" Oh, there was a tremendous energy of hatred in the mind and on the lips of the father as he gasped his last breath, thinking about how he could have had a son so despicable!

The son lived a good life. And it was also in his eighties that he passed on, surrounded by a family who loved him dearly, mourning for his essence that would no longer walk the planet. And this, dear ones, is where the story really begins. For the son passed to the cave of creation. He took the three-day journey where he picked up his essence and his name and moved on to the hall of honor. And he spent a long time in adoration there, where literally millions of entities, in a stadium that you cannot begin to fathom, applauded and honored him for what he had gone through while on your planet.

You see, dear ones, all of you have been there before, but we cannot show you this, for it would spoil your time here and give you too much remembrance. But you will be there again someday to pick up the next color. For these colors are seen by everyone in the universe when they meet you. Your colors are an identity badge indicating that you were a warrior of the light on the planet Earth. It is hard for you to conceive of, I know, at this moment as I tell you this story, but it is true, nonetheless.

You have no idea how important these unique Earth badges are. Someday you will remember my words when you meet me in the audience at the hall of honor.

And so, the son was there receiving his accolades, and his new colors were placed into his energy to spin into his other colors to show those around him who he was. And when this time was over, the son, in the cloak of the real universal entity that he was, entered into an area where he immediately saw his best friend Daniel—the one whom he had left to come to the planet Earth. And he saw Daniel from across the void and exclaimed, "It is you! I have missed you so!" And they came together, so to speak, and embraced, intermingling their energies. And so it was with great joy that they spoke about old universal times that they had enjoyed together before the son went to Earth.

Frolicking around the universe with his friend Daniel, one day he said to him, "You know, Daniel, you made a wonderful father on Earth."

"My best friend, you made a wonderful son," replied Daniel. "Wasn't it amazing what we went through as humans? How complete the duality was that separated us as best friends while we were on the Earth."

"How could something be like that?" the former son asked.

"Oh, it was because the veil was so strong that we didn't know who we really were," answered the former father.

"But the planning worked so well, didn't it?" asked the former son.

"Yes, it did," replied Daniel, "for we never once had a glimmer of truth as to who we really were!"

So we leave these two entities as they head toward the next Earth planning session. And we overhear one saying, "Oh, let's do it again! Only this time, I will be the mother, and you be the daughter!"

AUTHOR'S POSTSCRIPT:

*T*his precious story is told especially for some of you reading this now, who have yet to recognize the gift of what is taking place in your life—or have yet to recognize your best friend.

Look at the love it took for these entities to agree to go through this drama! The story gives you an example of anger and hatred, but they are only karmic attributes. They are fears to be broken, and I tell you now that had either the son or the father during their lifetime recognized who they were, they would have walked into the fear of the hatred and the anger, and come out with love. The other one could not have resisted it, and things would have been different for both of them. This is the new age human lesson. Regardless of what you think is in front of you and the way it appears, it may only be a paper-thin test ready to be dissolved and converted into love and peaceful compromise.

Do you have unresolvable anger at another? It's a trick of karma and a lesson for you, for you also know of the energy it takes to keep it going and the way it perpetuates itself seemingly without you. Isn't it time to release it?

Love is the greatest power of the universe. This love energy isn't just the thing that gives you peace and empowerment. Its energy is also responsible for your silence in the face of accusation—the wisdom and discernment to know that you helped plan everything around you. Strangely, this love is also responsible for the most unenlightened things that you can imagine, for the source of your karmic setup is also love. Sometimes it may take on an odd face, such as hate and anger towards a family member, but love is the king of the plan—and lurks waiting for you to discover it within the solution of your fear. It has substance and thickness. It has logic and reason. It is the essence of the universe, and it has been passed to you within the words of this story.

6

Sarah and the Old Shoe

AUTHOR'S NOTE:

Ready for a really short one? I love this parable because it represents how I think some of the time. I can really relate to becoming comfortable with...almost anything! Why change if things are working? What? You tell me IT ISN'T working? That's silly.

Sarah was a new age enlightened woman. She understood how to take responsibility for her life and that she was to find her reason for being on the planet. Sarah, therefore, asked her guides how to go about finding her "sweet spot" (the place where she agreed to be), and they gave her good information. She understood the processes and set about to co-create what she knew was her passion.

Sarah wished to be part of the ecology of the planet—to help with improving the Earth and all who lived on it. So, through a window of opportunity that suddenly appeared (a coincidence?), she was given the chance to do just that. The opportunity came in the form of a job within a company that worked with high-end ecological systems—something that excited Sarah greatly and made her feel that she could make a difference for many people. Her new job would take her across town each day to work in a comfortable office where she could accomplish her life's goal.

"This is why I am here," she acknowledged. "I have such a passion for this." She was elated and peaceful. Everything was working out fine as she started the job except for one thing. You see, coming into this incarnation on the planet, Sarah was given a fear of small places. In order to get to her job, it was necessary for Sarah to ride the subway train, and she was paralyzed twice a day by the experience. Each morning she would enter the subway and would slowly fry in her own fear. She would be anxious, gripping the pole with her sweaty hand, and her heart would pound for the entire 25 minutes it took to travel to this wonderful job.

After a month, Sarah came to her guides and painfully admitted, "This is not working for me. I need to find another job."

Her guides asked her, "How can this be? Didn't you co-create the exact situation you asked for? Is this not a victory?"

"I can't continue going to the job because of my fear of small places," replied Sarah. "It spoils my entire day—two times—coming and going!"

"Sarah," her guides suggested, "how about if we eliminate the fear, not the job."

"I don't know," replied Sarah hesitantly. "I've had the fear of small places for 35 years; I've only had the job for a month."

And so you see, Sarah was comfortable with her fear. Like an old shoe, it was somehow like a friend—a known quantity—something that was always there. And just like an old shoe, it might be ugly and tattered, but she had worn it for so long that it was the last thing she felt could be changed.

AUTHOR'S POSTSCRIPT:

*A*gain, this is a true story. Sarah is real, and the fear of small places, the job, and the problem is real. You will be pleased to know that Sarah walked into her fears, and to this day she rides the subway train in joy and peace to her wonderful job. But there was a time when she doubted it could happen. She would say, "What? This psychological problem has always been here. How could it ever leave? This is just too much to ask!"

Sarah finally decided that the job was more important than her fear, and she found to her amazement that her intent to void the claustrophobia was honored by God with almost immediate results. Just as her mind had a setup to create a fear of enclosed spaces, her mind also had the setup and ability to void it—and she took control of the situation and did exactly that! What a concept.

7

The Two Groups
of Warriors

AUTHOR'S NOTE:

This short little parable is one of my favorites. Much is hidden here regarding what we are supposed to do with the gifts of God in this new age.

It seems that there were two groups of warriors on a certain place on the planet Earth. Each group knew of the new gifts of God in the new age, and each group comprised warriors of the light. They understood their contracts and knew that there were dark forces at work that would like to prevent them from completing their personal goals. So they called on God for the gifts of the new energy, and each warrior received his package as requested.

Each package given to the warriors was personal, and each contained three items: a sword, a shield, and some body armor. The sword represented truth and could never be broken. Truth is pure, and the sword was, also, offering a perfect defense against the deceptions of the dark ones. The shield represented knowledge—knowledge of the weakness of the enemy, and knowledge from eons of archives from the ancients. No energy could penetrate the shield, since knowledge voided out secrets and conspiracy. Secrets and conspiracy cannot exist in the light of knowledge, for they depend on a dark place of ignorance for their power. The body armor represented the "mantle of the Spirit of God." This was the wisdom of spiritual awareness that gave humans the enablement as the "pieces of

God" that they are. Therefore, it represented the wisdom of God in all things—especially the wisdom to wield the truth and hold up the knowledge in the face of attack.

Now, it came to be that indeed there was a coordinated attack by the dark forces. Both groups of light warriors felt they were ready, and they quickly turned to their powerful gifts to ward off the enemy. As the dark forces closed in, the first group opened their packages and stared at the contents with disbelief. Everything was in parts! There was a manual with a note that said, "SOME ASSEMBLY REQUIRED." They couldn't begin to get ready in time to meet the enemy, and so this group of warriors was quickly overrun and was defeated at the hands of those who would control them. They became bitter and believed that God had tricked them into a false hope and sense of security. Oddly enough, even after defeat, they still had their packages, but they thought the tools were useless.

The other group had opened their packages long ago. They had put their tools together early, and they had practiced with them. It was a good thing they did, for they found the sword to be almost too swift to handle properly. They found the shield to have so many options that they had a difficult time knowing exactly how to hold it, and they found the body armor heavy indeed! With practice and meditation, they eventually learned how to balance everything, and they were ready.

They realized that no single tool worked without all three being engaged. The body armor, the closest thing to their skin, was the key, for it somehow gave them the wisdom to control the sword and the shield. Indeed, the shield was used in many modes depending on the situation, and the sword was easily controlled when the shield was used appropriately. When the attack came, the enemy took one look at this enabled force and fled. The battle was nonexistent, and the warriors rejoiced in their victory. There was no showdown, and no wounds were suffered.

———

AUTHOR'S POSTSCRIPT:

*T*here are some very spiritual people who continue to wait for God to "do something" for them. When they need healing, they ask God to do it, and they hope and hope and hope. When they wish to have situations around them change, they ask God to do it, and they wait and wait and wait. This comes squarely from the fact that this is the way it used to work, and the old scriptures show it. In fact, the story of Moses exemplifies this fact. God did everything, and Moses and his people were instructed to go when told to. From plagues to parting waters, to carving instructions in stone, everything was done by God. Even when the Israelites were wandering in the desert, God fed them daily, dropping food from heaven.

This was the old energy, before a time when we as humans were given permission to carry a greater energy and ability. When the great Jewish master of love, Jesus, walked our Earth, he was the messenger who gave us the word that everything was changing. The age of God's love was upon us. He spoke of spiritual gifts and showed them to us. He gave wonderful lectures, performed great miracles, showed a fisherman how to walk on water, and even spoke the words, "You can be just like me!" His message was clear: We are newly enabled spiritual creatures if we choose to be, with powers from the love source itself.

Now we find ourselves crowding the millennium, and more gifts are being given to us because, as Kryon tells it, we have earned them in this age of love. Even now, however, there are those who feel the old ways of waiting for God to do everything are still in effect—but they are not. In this new energy, we are asked to co-create our reality. Co-creation requires two entities (that's the "co" part). It requires cooperation between the God source and the God portion of the human called the "higher self."

We are absolutely required to learn the new ways of working spiritually in the new energy of our planet. The "doom and gloom" predictions of Nostradamus will come and go, and many will realize that Kryon was correct. We are in a brand-new paradigm for planet Earth, and as we sail past the time when everything was supposed to end, we'd better start understanding how we contribute spiritually to the entire scheme and find the designed ways to work with God to make this planet a grand place. Those who do not will be very disappointed, and they will not understand what happened.

Learn about the gifts. Pick up the package and use it! Understand how truth, knowledge, and wisdom work together to give great power in this new age!

8
Jason and the Cave

———•———

AUTHOR'S NOTE:

Here is a story about a game that was played between Jason and the guardian of the cave of creation. It's a test of self-control for Jason, disguised as a simple challenge. Can you guess the correlation to our lives?

———•———

Jason had a vision. Actually, it was a dream, but in Jason's case, there was no difference. Jason was very enlightened, and he often had visions in his dreams. This one was especially vivid.

Jason found himself at the opening of a great cave, and he instantly recognized what it was. This was the cave of creation, the site of the Akashic records, where all the details are kept regarding human entities entering and leaving the planet. Oh, I recognize this place! thought Jason to himself.

Standing at the cave was the guardian of the entrance. He did not seem bothered that Jason was suddenly standing at the entrance; in fact, he was expecting him! The guardian spoke. "Jason, it is good to see you here. We have a puzzle for you—a test—a game for your soul." The guardian smiled, and Jason knew some fun was at hand.

"This is wonderful," remarked Jason. "I love games."

"Take a look at the path," said the guardian as he effortlessly slid open the big door to the cave. Jason could see that there was a straight and narrow path through the cave. He could see at the other end of the cave that there was a light where the exit was. The cave was easily traversed.

"What is the game?" Jason asked the guardian.

"We would like you to walk through the cave to the exit, and we will give you one Earth hour to do so," said the guardian.

———— 39 ————

"No problem," replied Jason. "What do I get if I succeed?"

"This is not about reward. It is only in playing the game. There is great honor if you enter at all. Walking the path is the test, and making it to the exit is the goal. Can you do it?"

"I will succeed," said Jason, his sporting nature taking hold. And with that, the guardian stood aside, and Jason began his journey.

Jason entered the cave. Again, he looked ahead and saw that the exit was no more than a quarter-mile journey straight ahead. Realizing he had plenty of time, he stopped for a moment to let his eyesight become accustomed to the subdued lighting within the cave. He moved forward and was interested in the many colors he was seeing. It was not long before Jason also began hearing sounds. To the left and to the right of him, he heard events taking place. Jason thought to himself, I have an hour. It is only going to take me 15 minutes to get to the exit, so I shall stop and investigate what I am hearing.

Jason stopped and turned to the right. Instantly, he saw a rack full of glowing crystals. He carefully left the path and went over to the interesting objects. On each one of the wandlike crystals there was special writing. Jason gently grasped one, not picking it up. He was immediately taken to the event that the cryptic writing represented. Jason saw amazing things he never knew existed. He saw wars. He saw great conflagrations. He saw light against dark. He saw the names of so many entities. What an experience! He was actually there! Jason did not understand what he was seeing, but he marveled at the information and found it hard to release his grasp of the crystal—it was so compelling. Being mindful of the game and his limited time, Jason put the crystal down, still reeling with emotion at what he had just seen.

Back on the path, he realized that his crystal-touching experience had only taken a few moments. It seemed like so much longer! He was well within his time parameter. Jason moved forward on the path again, but in not too long a time he heard some voices, and he stopped. "What voice is this?" he said to himself. "I recognize it." Jason realized that it was his mother's voice! He turned to the left and saw another group of crystals not too far from him. He moved over to the group and somehow recognized his mother's crystal, but with a name etched upon it that was unfamiliar. He stayed for a moment, trying to hear what she was saying, but he could not. It had been years since she had passed on, and yet here she was—or was it only a crystal?

Jason had a choice. He knew he wanted to touch his mother's crystal. Something else said it was too private to do. Jason rationalized, "This is family, and she would want me to have her memory. Therefore, I am going to touch it." So, Jason touched the crystal, and immediately he was in the reality of the many lifetimes of his mother, and the Akashic records of her experiences on Earth unfolded before him. He saw the many lives she had and all of the years that she had spent on the planet and the years she had spent elsewhere, up to and including the one that he was in. Then he saw the one that she was in now as a child—that he was not a part of. It was fascinating, and he wept with remembrance and joy for her service. "Oh, this is wonderful! What a game is this!" he said out loud in the cave. And with some difficulty, he took his hand away, only to realize that the crystal next to it was his father's. And so Jason touched that as well, and he had a similar experience there, and he said again, "This is wonderful. What a study this is. I am so honored. I am so honored."

Time was now growing short. Jason knew he had to move on or he would not make it to the exit in time. So Jason started quickly down the path and proceeded to within a few feet of the exit when he heard another voice. This time he recognized that it was his own!

Jason turned to the right, and there was another crystal glowing. On this one he recognized the name, for there was a private spiritual name etched into the crystal in what looked to Jason like Arabic letters, which spelled his astral name. Jason looked at the exit of the cave a few feet away—with full knowledge that he only had a few moments left. Then he looked at his crystal and made up his mind. He simply could not pass up this opportunity. He turned to the right and touched the crystal with his name on it. Needless to say, Jason did not make it out of the cave in the allotted time for the game to be complete. He stayed there, reveling in his own past lives with great understanding of who he was and who he was supposed to be, with tremendous understanding of the overview of who his mother and father were in his past lives and who he was in their lives as well. And then Jason awoke.

Jason thought, What a wonderful dream this has been! Then he remembered all of it. "But I am sorry I did not win the game," he lamented. So, Jason went forward with his life, not understanding what the dream really meant, but feeling no judgment from the guardian. Occasionally he thought, If I could play it again, it would be different. I know the pitfalls now.

Jason did not understand that he was in the game still.

—————

AUTHOR'S POSTSCRIPT:

*M*any who read this little story feel that the path though the cave is a person's life, and that the exit is the end of life. Actually, Kryon's explanation is that the path is indeed life, but the exit represents illumination, self-realization, enlightenment, and a change in the future. Therefore, the parable represents a human being with a seemingly straightforward task: Walk the path from the start to the finish without spending too much time looking around—and you will get there. Really, there is much more information here. Kryon tells us that we are the exalted ones walking the planet, and that while we are here, we tend to feel the opposite and spend a great deal of time studying the past.

I quote from Kryon Book II, *page 204: "Kryon wants us to know that if the star player of the game becomes enthralled and stands motionless in awe of his teammates...that the game will never get played, much less won. We are to gather information as tools for our own action. We are never to study the members of our support group to the extent that it stops our own development."*

Past-life regression is great unless you tend to live in the past all the time. Studying the history of the metaphysical universe is enlightening unless that's all you do. Kryon recognizes that there is more information available on these subjects than at any time in the history of the world—and it's fascinating information due to our new powers of discernment and intuition. However, if the goal in life is to discover our personal reasons for being here, to raise the vibration of the planet, and to move forward with self-realization, then we cannot spend all of our time looking at what was.

What would you have done if you were Jason? Would you have stopped when you found your crystal? I know I would have. Sometimes the distractions are almost irresistible. I guess that's why God calls what we are doing "work."

9
Jessica the Angry

AUTHOR'S NOTE:

The transmutation of anger and fear to peace and joy are the favorite subjects of Kryon's stories. Here is a story that many women will relate to, for it is a real-life situation that many have experienced—and still do. Men, take note, for it might help you to relate to your life partner better.

Jessica was a very sweet woman, but she was also extremely angry. Deep within her sweet exterior there was a seething anger that perpetuated itself at every opportunity. It was mad, vindictive, and destructive. It was also self-defeating and shouted to Jessica's mind that she was unworthy to be alive.

Very few got to see Jessica's anger under her sweet exterior. On the outside, she appeared to be one way, but on the inside she was another, and the anger seemed to come out in the worst places and at the worst times. These outbursts only seemed to make her more angry—as if she were angry about being angry! The last thing Jessica wanted in the world was for her countenance to be one of anger, so she hid it whenever she could, knowing that it was not becoming to a gentle female in her culture.

Relationships were a disaster for Jessica. Each time she would end one herself with explosive anger—and the man would not return. She could not help herself. Perhaps angry at something or nothing, Jessica was uncertain, but angry she was. After that, she would become sweet again, until the next situation where the buttons were pressed and the anger would come out. It was vivid and it was ugly, and she was out of control and knew it.

Jessica sought help, and it was not long before she realized that her anger was due to what happened when she was a child, for Jessica had been abused. The way her father had treated her emotionally was inexcusable! The things done in the name of biological lust were also inexcusable! Every time she would think of those times, there would be more anger. How she hated him! Jessica had escaped from her home life as soon as she could, and she never saw her father again. Much to the distress of her now-deceased mother, she could never talk about why she left in such an angry manner. Mom hadn't been part of the problem, she thought, and yet it separated them as well. Jessica was angry about that, too. Her mom never got to be the friend that some women experienced later in life.

As it happened, Jessica's search for self-help turned into genuine enlightenment. She met a woman friend who expressed the joy, love, and peace that Jessica longed for so much. The woman introduced her to some startling concepts of self-worth and responsibility that really made sense but that were still hard for her to grasp. Jessica realized, however, that there was more to life than to walk around with this anger, and she hoped so much that this woman's new belief system would help her void this anchor of anger and allow her to get rid of it once and for all.

And so, on her new enlightened path, she asked her angels and guides one night, "What can I do to void this anger? What can I do?"

And her angels stood before her and said, "Find your father and face him!"

AAHHGH! Those were the worst words that Jessica could ever hear. And so the blackness of fear came upon her. To find her father and see his face again was the last thing she ever wanted to do! She was even angry at her angels that they would suggest such a thing. She had spent night after night running the scenario in her mind of how to get away from the memory of him—now the angels said to find him? NO!

And so she asked again, "Angels and guides, what can I do to find peace?"

"Find your father and face him!" they still replied. And again, she felt the blanket of fear come over her. As if she were a child again, she could see her father's black and terrible lusty eyes. In her mind, she could smell the alcohol, and she was extremely afraid. Nevertheless, Jessica eventually did what she was told. She said to herself, "I will walk into this, my bleakest place of existence—my father's actions that ruined my life. I don't know what it will do for me, but I am going to honestly try to do it."

She sought out her father and found, much to her disappointment, that he was still in town. It would have been easier for her if he could not have been found, but that was not the case. So, indeed, her fears would have to be realized. Jessica thought to herself, I will wait until a time when I feel he will be home, when he's not yet drunk. I can see myself at his door. I will knock without fear, and when he answers, I will tell him what I think! I will tell him how awful it was—what he did to me. I will let him know that he is responsible for ruining life with Mom, ruining my childhood, ruining my life with other men! I'm going to read him up one side and down the other. Then I will be free.

But a funny thing happened to Jessica the night before the event. As God often does, there was an 11th-hour intervention. Like the angel who stayed the hand of Abraham as he was about to face his worst fear, so it was that Jessica was given a remarkable vision. She was taken away in this vision and shown who her father truly was. She saw the overview. She saw two best friends making a contract before ever coming to Earth. She got to see the role of her father's entity in her own past lives—as a loving past mate in the last; a wonderful, caring sister in a lifetime before that; and a good friend before that. She saw that both of them had fulfilled their contracts on the planet. For he had come in and committed despicable acts and had been forced to live with them. She had come in and been abused and had to live with that. As best friends with the mind of God, they had penned their lives together in a contract of appropriateness before they ever got here, and they were now living out the play on Earth as designed by both of them.

The reality of the vision profoundly affected Jessica. Could it be so? Was this all a test between disguised angelic friends? As if being answered, she felt a tremendous wash of love from her angels, and she knew it was so. Jessica knew she was free. She knew her anger was no more because she got to see the overview of love surrounding the purpose for her life experience. The father had facilitated the anger of her test, just as planned. Now she could see the phantom of her fear and how it could no longer stand under the exposure of truth. The anger had been disconnected, and she felt totally disengaged from the fear surrounding her dad. Just her intent to face the fear was enough—just like Abraham's pure intent to do as he was told was enough.

Now Jessica, at that point in time, had the option to decide not to go through with the actual confrontation of her father. She knew her task was complete, and she had walked directly into her fear. She had given perfect intent to do the work of meeting him, and she had been honored by the giving of the vision. She had the overview and the wisdom of God. She had disarmed a life lesson, and she now felt incredible peace.

But Jessica felt compelled in love to go the final route. With her newfound strength and lack of anger or vindictiveness, she went to her father's door and rang the bell. When he came to the door, she saw a beaten man, looking far older than his age. He had lost all his hair, and there was shock in his eyes when he recognized her. As she stood in front of him, there was a welling up of emotion in his eyes. Before he could speak, she said to him earnestly, "Father, I love you. Thank you for doing what you came to do. You are forgiven in every single way. I am your daughter, who is now peaceful in her life." Without another word, she left him standing there alone to ponder how such a thing could be.

Jessica could have no way of knowing that her father was a depressed and despondent man. Long ago he had given up his abusive habits just to stay alive, but his life was sorrowful, and he felt unworthy to live. You see, within his life, he had his own self-worth problems. He had played out his part and was wallowing in the horror of it all. He knew that what he had done had been unforgivable, and yet he dreamed nightly about a sweet daughter who would eventually come to him so he could beg forgiveness. He didn't have the strength to find her, and he greatly feared her rejection if he did so. He had dreamed of his daughter coming to his door and saying, "Father, I forgive you." And now it had happened. He was never the same, and shortly he was able to laugh again. His prayers had been answered. He had been forgiven by the only human entity in God's plan who could do it, and he began to feel worthy again.

That night, two lives were saved—saved from the dark negativity and fear that had encased both of them for so long, all due to the wise actions of an enlightened daughter. Many years later, two good angel friends would frolic in the stars, telling their tale of when they were father and daughter and how they had beaten the test and recognized who they were while in human form. They told of how the truth can never hide when you ask it to be revealed, and how the love of God always prevails over the dark.

AUTHOR'S POSTSCRIPT:

*C*an we really eliminate lifelong fears or years of anger through self-realization? Ask Jessica, for the story is real, and her victory is real. A letter that I received after the live session with Kryon confirmed that the story was about one who was actually attending. Many men and women have come to understand that there is no victimization involved in being abused. The setup is in place, and the test is what a person is going to do with the often-disabling attributes of anger and fear. Do you let these emotions consume you and control your actions, or do you ask God to help you find out what the test is?

Discovery of self includes discovery of why you are here and why it all happened. Did you ever ask yourself, "Why me?" The real answer might blow you away! What if the answer was: "Because you planned it"? Kryon says that in the middle of the worst fear and anger is also the greatest release of love possible. The tests are hard, but the rewards of passing through them are filled with splendor and hope. Are you capable of such a thing? Absolutely. Kryon tells us that only the most worthy are here to walk the tests of this planet.

10
The Infant's Questions

AUTHOR'S NOTE:

Almost every mom I know with an infant has secretly wished that she could have a fluent two-way adult conversation with this precious entity. There is so much to tell a child! See if you can glean the real meaning of the following parable about a magic conversation between a mother and her infant son. It's a fun story with an important message.

The human mother was startled indeed when the large male angel appeared in her laundry room. "What are you doing here?!"

"You expected me in the kitchen?" asked the angel.

"No, I didn't expect you at all!" the mother answered. "Why are you here?"

"To grant your request," said the angel, as if it were a common thing to appear in a human's home.

"I don't remember any request!" exclaimed the mother. "I hope I asked for something good and that you didn't just overhear me swearing. I say things all the time when I'm mad."

"No, no," replied the angel. "Remember when you were looking into the eyes of your son and murmured, 'If only we could talk to each other'? Well, I'm here to arrange that. Tomorrow night when you go into your son's nursery, I will be there to allow you to speak to him, and he to you. You will have a brief time where he can speak to you with the intellect of an adult and the language of an adult. I'll tell you more when I see you then." And with that, the angel disappeared—slightly to the left of the dryer—and up a vent.

The mother was not frightened. After all, she believed in angels and had been to the local angel shop many times. She had no way of knowing that real angels don't like angel shops. All the popularity had taken the fun out of appearing before people. Some mothers even wanted to know where the angel got its costume—very insulting to a real live angel.

The mother didn't sleep much that night, and when she put her six-month-old infant to bed early in the evening, she looked deep into his eyes and said, "Tomorrow you and I will actually get to speak to each other!" She was excited indeed. He drooled in response.

She carefully crafted what she would say to him. Where does one begin? How long would she have? Would she be able to communicate the difficult things of life? She started by thinking of all the things she wanted to tell a child just starting out in life—about how a stove is hot, and a pretty fire can hurt—but wait! The angel said the child would speak with an adult's mind. That would change everything! She would need to tell him how to handle girls, and how to treat a broken heart, and how not to trust everyone, and how not to drive too fast. Oh my! There is so much to tell him about being human, she thought.

The next evening, the time for the magic discussion slowly approached. She waited with her infant son at her side in the nursery until the appointed hour, when the angel appeared again.

"Nice to see the both of you," the angel quickly said. "Here are the rules of the conversation. Mom, you can only answer. Son, you can only ask three questions. Then it's over." And with that, the angel again disappeared—this time down the furnace grate.

This changes everything, thought the mother in silence while looking at her son. Perhaps I am hallucinating. I'll bet my son simply goes to sleep now. Instead, the infant stood up!

"Mother," said the infant. "it's a magical day indeed that brings us together like this. What a joy to be able to speak to you at this point in my life!"

The mother stood up at attention—with her mouth dropping in amazement. She even drooled a bit.

"Only three questions can I ask," the boy continued from the crib. "I want to know so much!" The boy was thinking about his first question as his mother was taking it all in. This is real, she thought. My son is talking to me as if he were all grown up! What a miracle. What a gift. She could hardly contain herself waiting for her son's first question. Would it be about philosophy or religion? Perhaps he would want to know the best advice to guide him into a good career, or maybe he wanted to know how he should choose the best mate—one who would stick around longer than hers did. The boy looked into his mother's eyes and asked the first question.

"Mother, I have laid outside this house on my back and was amazed at the sky. Why is it blue?"

It was all the mother could do not to shout: "You wasted the first question! Who cares why the sky is blue!" But the mother was so in love with her son that she patiently answered the question according to the rules. She explained how the atmosphere and oxygen molecules refract the light of the sun and turn it blue—at least that's what she believed. It sounded good, anyway. She anxiously waited for the next question. The next one has to be better, she thought. Perhaps he would like to know what he should do with his life in order not to end up homeless or with delinquent friends.

"Mother, my second question is this. Although I have been here only six months, I notice that sometimes it is hot outside, and sometimes it is cold. Why is that?"

The mother was appalled. Another question wasted on dumb stuff! How could this be, she wondered. Her son was innocent and alert. His question was important to him, and she treasured this magic time they could have together. Slowly, she tried to tell him about the Earth and the sun, and how the Earth tilts slightly as it orbits the sun, causing winter and summer, cold and hot. Finally, it was time for the last question. They had been at it for almost 30 minutes, and so little had actually been communicated.

"Mother, I love you!" exclaimed the son. "But how do I know you are really my mother? Do you have some kind of proof?"

What kind of a question was this? Where did that come from? Who else would be his mother? Hadn't she cared for him every day of his life? What a disappointment this session had been. She almost wanted to walk away and go back to the laundry room where this had all started. She thought of how she was going to shove the angel in the dryer the next time she saw him. Her son, his innocent eyes wide open and alert, was waiting for a reply.

She started crying, but held out her hands and said, "Look at my fingers; they are just like yours. My feet and my face look like yours. My expressions of joy and love are just like yours. I am truly your mother. We have the same eyes and mouth—look!" With that, the child was satisfied, and he slowly laid himself down on his mat and went to sleep.

That was it? This miracle of communication had come and gone, and the mother had not had a meaningful conversation with her beautiful son. What happened? What went wrong? She spent a great deal of time thinking about it all, and she mourned the passing of such an event without anything substantive being transferred.

Then the angel appeared again—up through the bathroom drain.

"Go away," the mother said before the angel could say anything. "What a disappointment you turned out to be."

"I gave you the time," the angel said kindly. "I did not design the questions."

"What good was it? Why didn't my son ask anything important? You told me he would have the mind of an adult, but he asked the questions of a child. You have tricked me with your so-called miracle."

"Dear one," the angel replied, "although your son was given the language and the intellect of an adult, he had only the wisdom and experience of the six months he had been on Earth. His questions were therefore the most meaningful ones he could think of, and you answered them all. Even the last one, which was postured in fear, you answered correctly. In addition, you transmitted your love to him while you were together, and you were not impatient with him. He did his best and was honest. What more could you ask?"

The mother sat down. She hadn't thought of that. Her son had mustered up the best questions he could come up with. How could he know what to ask if he didn't have the wisdom she had? And if he had somehow been given that wisdom, he would not have had to ask anything! Without any more communication, the angel left for the final time—this time out the window.

The mother returned to the crib and spent a long time looking at her precious son. "You did your best, my son," she said in a quiet voice. "It was good that we had time for a talk."

AUTHOR'S POSTSCRIPT:

So, did you get the real meaning of this fun little story? You and I do not have the mind of God while we are here on the planet, and yet we have the gift of being able to speak with the masters. How patient they must be with us as we flounder around with questions that have no bearing on the real reasons we are here. How can we know what to ask? Kryon gave us the magic question right after this story was given in live session (coming in a moment).

The interesting thing about this story is that God answers our questions even if they are meaningless to our lives or to the planet's purpose. Have you ever read a book about the lineage of the vast amount of entities around us? There are some books that give you chapter and verse— the names and the battles and how Earth came to be. It tells who the players were and what happened to them long before there was even an atmosphere on the planet. And if you read these books, did they give you a warm, fuzzy feeling inside? Did they make you understand what to do with your life? Do you now have a clear direction about which way to turn to solve the problems of being a human in this new age? I'll bet not. Your book just gave you the answer to the metaphysical child's question, "Why is the sky blue?"

So many times we are compelled to ask God to prove that God is God. Show me this and show me that. How can I know you are real? How can I know you are God? This is when "made in His image" is often explained, and it's when we get to understand the metaphor of love, with the "image of God" being the imprint of love and compassion we each come in with. Think of how insulting this question is for the angels and for the exalted ones who have been at our side from birth, and yet the answers are always compassionate and loving. Even these answers, however, don't get us from A to B, nor do they help us through unsatisfying relationships, meaningless jobs, health problems, financial issues, or family and community difficulties.

Kryon tells us that there is only one real question that can make a difference in our lives and change us dramatically. When we sit before God in meditation and prayer, there is a two-way communication going. Some say that prayer is when we speak to God, and meditation is when we listen. The next time you have the opportunity to speak and listen, ask the following question:

"Dear God, what is it you wish me to know?"

There is no greater question than this, and it reflects your wisdom of spiritual awareness like no other. If the child had asked this, the mother would still be answering to this day, and the child would have been far wiser in his growth.

11
Marla the Mouse

AUTHOR'S NOTE:

I was in Seattle before a large crowd of very intense, serious metaphysical people when Kryon decided to give them a children's story! I cringed, but began it anyway as directed. Kryon said that the metaphysical elite who were gathered there knew very well that young people have many of the childlike attributes of a number of the ascended masters. Therefore, we bring you a story about a mouse.

Marla the Mouse was a good mouse who lived with many mice in a mouse city. Marla had many things to eat and lived a fine mouse life. Along the way, Marla had many dreams that she did not understand. She had dreams where she seemingly soared in the air and where she felt different, and she just did not understand these dreams. So Marla, being an inquisitive mouse, called upon God-mouse and said, "Squeak squeak." (We will interpret.)

"What are these dreams of mine, for they interest me greatly?" asked Marla. Suddenly, in front of Marla, two mouse-angels appeared with their furry wings.

"Marla, we wish to show you what your dreams mean," said the mouse-angels. "Come with us if you choose, and we will take you on an important path."

"Yes, I would like to go!" replied Marla.

"You will be away from the others for a time," squeaked the mouse-angels, "and there will be difficulties, for there are mountains to climb."

"That's okay. I am going with you," Marla squeaked excitedly.

And so the mouse-angels took Marla by the paw and started their journey. She left the mouse city, and the mouse-angels were correct, for there were times when Marla wanted to turn back. As easily as it would have been for her to tuck her tail between her legs and return, she did not. She continued to move forward a day at a time despite the difficulties.

Along the way, Marla noticed that there were other mice who had joined the journey, asking the same questions as Marla had. Each additional mouse was added along the trail, some in higher places than Marla had started from. Some mice dropped out of the journey, feeling that it was too difficult. Some missed their friends and family in the city and decided to go back. Even so, there were many mice following the mouse-angel guides to find out about the wonderful dreams they were having.

Finally, they reached the top of a magnificent precipice. It had taken them a long time to get there, but they were not tired, for they were very anxious to know what their dreams had meant. All of the mice intuitively knew that there was some hidden message within the dreams, something special, something magnificent—and they were not disappointed.

They lined up on the precipice and saw before them a grand ocean, a body of water that they were unaware of. Marla had never seen an ocean before and was mouse-awed. Oh, it smelled wonderful. Marla had never smelled anything so inviting as the salt of the ocean. They were all very excited, for they knew something was about to change.

"We have information for you that will now make sense of your dreams," said the mouse-angels. "You are not mice at all. You are fish!" Marla was astounded at this information, but she was pensive for a moment.

"I'm not sure I want to be a fish," said Marla to any mouse listening. But then the mouse-angels showed her the kind of fish that they meant. It was a hundred times the size of Marla. A grand, silvery, sparkling, magnificent, glowing fish! She was again mouse-awed by this sight. Then she realized that the dreams she had were of being a fish—soaring to the heights, hundreds of feet in the ocean, above and below, totally free, with big, wonderful fish muscles! One flip of a tail would send the fish many,

many yards. What freedom to float through the water! Then Marla felt that this, indeed, is where she came from. This was home!

And as if all of them realized it together, the mice suddenly looked over the ocean to see that there were fish there, sticking their heads out, waving flippers at them, saying, "Remember us, we were your mouse friends from before."

Marla recognized a few of them and said, "Yes, I didn't know where you went! Now I know."

And then the guides told the group an amazing thing. "Not only is this the interpretation of your dreams, but your journey to this place has a reward as well. Just by asking, you can be a magnificent fish, also, and you can jump into this ocean, join your friends, and live an expanded life. The choice is yours."

Marla watched as three of her mouse friends instantly did exactly that. What a miracle! It was almost as if they shed their mouse costumes and dove into the great sea. Then Marla had a thought, and she asked her mouse-angels, "What about the others—the ones we left behind in the city? Will they come as well?"

"No," replied the wise mouse-fish-angels. "This is not for every mouse. They must ask as you did and be as aware as you were about their inner quests."

"How will they know about this?" asked Marla.

"Through dreams, and mouse-enlightenment" said the mouse-fish-angels.

Then Marla asked an important question. "If I were to return and help them with mouse-enlightenment, could I still be a fish?"

"Anytime you wish," answered the mouse-fish-angels. "In fact, you can be a fish now and help them in the city as well."

"How can I be in two places at the same time?" inquired Marla. "Won't my fish presence scare them?"

"Consider it the beginning of mouse-fish-angel training! You will understand it all soon. If you go back as a fish, some will reject you, for they will not see the fish part of you. They will only see you as different and odd. It's a difficult thing being in two places at the same time. It's up to you Marla—will you join us?" The mouse-fish-angels then turned into fish and disappeared into the ocean with the others.

———

Now this is the point in a children's story where we tell you everything turned out fine and that Marla lived happily ever after as a fish. But in this tale, the mouse-angels had asked Marla for a decision, and that is where we leave the story.

Dear ones, we wish you to understand the point of "Marla the Mouse." In the new enlightened energy, some of you will have two pulls upon you: one will be to change and join the others in a graduate status while remaining on the planet; the other will be to stay as you are and do good work for humanity. Not all are called to this place. Make no mistake. Whatever is your decision is honored without judgment. Each one of you is alone in this and will know what to do. So the answer to what Marla did lies within your own heart. Such is the process of being an ascended one in the new energy.

———

AUTHOR'S POSTSCRIPT:

*T*his parable exemplifies one of the most powerful and elite gifts of the new age—ascension status. It can also be the most confusing. Many have felt that this new gift is where humans can go through a process of vibratory change and actually ascend into the heavens, never to be seen again. This, indeed, is an option.

Kryon tells us, however, that true new age ascension status is where humans remain on the planet in a new vibratory state. We stay human, but with the attributes of an ascended one. He also tells us that the path is difficult, but that it is honored and not for all humans to do. It is all part of the energy and vibration that this planet will need to move into the new millennium. We will need to have a certain amount of ascended ones walking among us who have the vibratory rate from the other side of the veil, while remaining on Earth. They will not necessarily be welcomed either, for the lower vibration of most of us will not mix well with the high vibrations of the ascension status. It is a role, therefore, requiring some sacrifice.

The fish example? It's who we are when we are not here. It's our natural state in the ocean of the cosmos. Can we be a fish and remain in human form (or mouse form)? Yes, we can, and that's the challenge of the ascension status. With the challenge, however, comes the certainty that to do so will cause a distance from many of our friends and family, who don't know of such things and vibrate differently. Because of the change in you, some will even call you evil. This status is beginning to be exposed by many enlightened teachers and will be clearer as time goes on. Kryon chose to tell this as a children's story in order to begin instruction on a complicated subject—and in a way we could all relate to.

12
Angenon and Veréhoo

AUTHOR'S NOTE:

One of Kryon's favorite subjects has to do with the trials of women in our culture and what the lessons mean personally for them. Kryon is not a "he" or a "she" any more than God is. Kryon's entity is that of a master of human understanding who is giving us loving information regarding the new age. As a male, I was uncomfortable at first about translating Kryon's words, which often seemed so personally directed toward women. Now, I not only feel comfortable but understand the joke. We all get our turn, and chances are that all the men reading this will relate at some level—since our lineage of lifetimes would naturally encompass many female incarnations as well. In the translations of these stories, I also got to feel in whatever capacity I could, what it was like to have some of the problems that only a female could experience in our society. This has tempered me and made me a wiser man.

This story is told from the perspective of two angel guides (something that Kryon has done before). Their guide names were given as Angenon and Veréhoo. I put an accent mark on Veréhoo, since it was given to me as VER (sounds like "fur")-A (as in "hay")-HOO. They are the guides of a woman named Wo. As you read this book, you will discover that Wo is in two other parables. "Is it the same Wo?" you might ask. Indeed it is, but as told here, Wo is in another life.

Angenon and Veréhoo were guides. Angenon was different, for he had been a human before, so he carried the stripe of the human. Veréhoo had never been human and had always been of the angel-guide group. Both of them had been with humans lifetime after lifetime, and both Angenon and Veréhoo were excited. They were on their way to another planning session that marked the beginning of yet another human's life— always a festive time.

They were going to meet their assigned entity shortly—one of those who would be sent to the Earth-plane as the guardian of love, a human scheduled to be a warrior of the light. These two guides, Angenon and Veréhoo, standing side by side going into the planning session, were going to meet the entity we call Wo. We heard of Wo before, in a previous parable given one year ago in this very room.

Wo stands now in the chamber of planning, close to the portal leading to the cave of creation. Wo is ready to pick up his essence and return with his karma intact to the planet Earth. Angenon and Veréhoo are part of the planning, and here it is that Wo and all the others plan the lessons generated by the karma (past lives) and the current experiences they will have. The planning is clear but is not to be confused with predestination. Again, Wo will come into the Earth-plane where he will be exposed to the appropriate karma, and he will have his chance to walk through it (just as he had in the past). This is done to give Wo a chance to raise the vibration of the planet through his efforts.

So Wo is prepared in this planning session to pick up where he left off (karma-wise) and return to Earth. Here, Wo plans with other entities yet to come into lesson—and with the higher souls of those already on Earth walking in lesson. So it was that the formerly male Wo decided to come back with Angenon and Veréhoo, this time as a Wo-man. The guides willingly began their journey to come to Earth with her, and so it was also that she chose the attribute to be born on the first day of the month of September (she is going to have a difficult time with control)!

In the first years of life, Wo is abused by her father, abused by her stepfather, and even abused by her stepfather's brother. By the time she is

11 years old, she carries the heavy karma of a long cycle—by design. During this time, Angenon and Veréhoo stand beside her, watching her preplanned karma of choice develop.

Dear ones, there is no such thing as predestination. Your lessons are decided and set in advance, but the solutions are yours while you are on Earth. It is thus: If you were to send entities down to Earth as hammers and visited them some years later, you would not be surprised to find them in the company of nails. This is logic, not predestation. So the attributes of the ones who are born September 1 are known, and you will not be surprised at the problems they encounter or the lessons that they must walk through.

Wo has a difficult time with males. She has no problems with abundance, for this is not the karma she carries. Money seems to come easily to her, and in the area of Earth business, she delights in her quest to rise to the top. She becomes spiteful due to the anger and energy of her karmic lesson, and she devours the spirit of males around her—enjoying the game of business and of winning over her male counterparts. She tried partnerships three times, but none were able to survive—due to her anger. As Wo grew older, her health became poor, and her imbalance allowed for stress-related disease.

Angenon and Veréhoo watched in love, quietly knowing that all was appropriately set for the next stage, for Wo and the others had decided that this could be a very important incarnation, one to remember due to the Earth's new attributes. It was in Wo's 47th year that she was "accidentally" exposed to an enlightened woman—in one of those business intensives where humans are forced together for a week, unable to escape (in the name of efficiency). Angenon and Veréhoo both recognized the woman, for it was an entity from the same planning session that they had attended 47 years earlier. This was the one who was scheduled to appear this year, and if Wo was ready, to inform her of God's gifts in the new age.

As fate would have it, Wo was interested in this woman. Wo wanted to know what was different about her; and as if by fate (cosmic joke), Wo approached the woman late one night and asked the questions, "Why is it you have peace? How are you so tolerant of men? What is your secret?"

Angenon and Veréhoo were on their toes! Poised in the balance of a moment was everything they had waited for. They both sensed the potency of what was happening, and they knew that this was the prime window of opportunity that they had been preparing for. Never in the history of their guide assignments had anything like this happened! As the woman spoke of truth, Wo remained stoic, taking it all in. Later that night it happened. Alone in her room, she openly wept, raised her hands in apparent desperation, and verbally asked if God would grant her an audience. As if the light were suddenly turned on, Angenon and Veréhoo were put into action. She had expressed intent! Yes! The universe was listening. Yes! There was something else grander than the human intellect, and yes! she could have peace during her incarnation. Angenon and Veréhoo celebrated, and it caused Wo a very sleepless night to have all that activity around her bed!

Things started changing quickly for Wo. She met with the woman many more times and became fast friends with her. She met others who took her through processes and gave her information she needed. All the time, Angenon and Veréhoo were rejoicing in the new communication they were allowed to have with Wo and her higher God-self. Later, a third angel-guide from a master guide group joined Angenon and Veréhoo, and so it was that Wo was able to walk directly into her karma and forgive those who had harmed her so. And so it was that she gained wisdom and realized her responsibility for all that had happened. And with her WISDOM came LOVE. And with the LOVE came ACTION! Then came a time when Wo not only was able to tolerate the males in her life, but actually partnered with one—successfully and lovingly. This was quite amazing, considering who Wo "used to be."

In Wo's 53rd year, Angenon and Veréhoo were required to leave. Wo had become of such a vibration that a totally new set of guides was needed to best serve her. As her set of guides retreated from her for a period of 90 days, Wo was without support, but even under this stress, Wo understood what was happening and quietly busied herself with other human things, and she got through this period without difficulty.

Angenon and Veréhoo celebrated again. You might have thought that Wo's angel friends would have been unhappy, that they would have felt sorrow and grief at having to depart from a much-loved friend—one whom they had waited for and planned for, for so long! But Angenon and Veréhoo knew that the parts were in balance, and the graduation of the one exalted the whole, so they willingly departed without rebellion or even a thought of anything but love for the process.

We leave Wo there, because her future has not been realized yet—much like your own.

————

AUTHOR'S POSTSCRIPT:

*I*n this story, Wo is a "she," and the entire story is told from the perspective of the guides. This parable contains important information regarding the working of the guides. Remember that in earlier writings, Kryon has told us of the fact that we all come in with at least two guides who are always with us, that some of us get a third, and that with the enlightenment there is the potential of a full guide change. This full guide change is often a 90-day challenge that he has spoken of before.

Right away, Kryon lets us know about the two guides who are going to be assigned to "Wo." One guide has been human before, and one has not. This information would indicate that humans don't always come back as humans. Did you ever wonder if your "guardian angel" was someone you used to know? This story provides evidence that it could actually be that way! The information is that the angel guides are specialists in service to support us in lesson, and that the guide group contains those who were always guides and others who were humans.

The next bit of information is that the guides are with us when the contracts are planned. Kryon has told us from the start that we are part of the God energy—that we, while in God consciousness (something that humans can't understand fully), plan our own incarnations and the opportunities for lessons within them.

This, by the way, makes us totally responsible for absolutely everything that happens to us along the way, since we have been told through countless messages that "there are no accidents" and that "coincidence" isn't.

So the guides are going to the planning meeting to meet the human they will accompany and to actually plan the opportunities for the next life! This is wonderful information, and it helps us to understand why the guides are important—for they stand by to implement plans that we all helped make.

Kryon also wants us to once again recognize the difference between what is going on in this planning session in regard to predestination. Predestination is a human concept and is not a spiritual reality. Our planning sessions are only setups of lessons. In other words, when you are in school at your desk, you can do anything you want with the test in front of you: throw it away, make a paper airplane and fly it out the window, or muster up some energy and pass it! It's totally up to you. In this case, the test was written by you when you were in "God consciousness," but you don't recognize this fact at all. Can you see how this differs greatly from predestination? We have total free choice all the time. Kryon's humor again shows itself with his analogy of hammers and nails surrounding his explanation of how the planning works.

The next piece of startling information is that the planning session includes the "higher souls of those already on Earth walking in lesson." Take a look at this! It's the first indication from Kryon that karmic planning involves those already living and walking around. This is how the "engine" of group karma is therefore facilitated. In other words, if the karmic planning committee always had to wait for humans to pass on before the next incarnations were planned, it would be very inefficient. Entities would be literally "standing around," waiting for the others to die before they could plan how to interact with them the next time.

Think about it—you interact karmically with parents and children; therefore, there are big age differences. So this explains how it can be that a child could come into the world and die sadly, but appropriately, for the lesson of the parents, and then come in again shortly thereafter as still another child of the same parents (if appropriate). I say this not to indicate that God has this scenario happen, but to show how the planning works.

How can the planning involve the living, you might ask? Kryon has told us on many occasions of the "oversoul" or "higher self" of each of us. In fact, the quest of your enlightenment and ascension is to marry to your higher self and stick around the planet as a power worker (see the parable in this book called "Marla the Mouse"). Evidently, this higher self is part of us, in contact with God all the time, but whose energy is not totally in our bodies. Therefore, there is still communication with God on karmic things (at least). This also helps explain how the complex interactions of karma can continue to change as those around us work through their karma, and we work through ours. In other words, we alter the lesson plan as we pass each test. Part of us is keeping score!

The story sets up Wo as an abused child who is harmed by many men who are supposed to be part of her family support group. This is given to help you see how the abandonment karma is set up and what kind of personality type might result. Evidently, Wo becomes an overachieving woman with no financial problems, but one who has a lot of trouble with men. (No wonder!) She likes to win at business, and she enjoys competition with men (the actual translation was that she likes to beat them at their own game). She has three failed marriages or relationships of some kind, and she carries around a great deal of anger, which later gives her stress-related health problems.

Now, where were Angenon and Veréhoo all this time? What good is all this guardian angel stuff if they don't do anything to help someone in this type of mess? Well, these questions are joke questions, since the reality is that "Angenon and Veréhoo watched in love, quietly knowing that all was appropriately set for the next stage . . ." All 47 years of this woman's life were a setup to a great test that was coming. Think of it—the patience of the angels!

The "scheduled one" arrived on the scene. The guides recognized her instantly and got excited. Reading on, this scheduled person who came into Wo's life was actually part of the contract planning session 47 years earlier. Think of the complexity of this! In her own way, Wo recognized the woman, too, because it says that Wo was interested in her and the things she had to say. Here was a woman who was different—the tar wasn't sticking to her! This is a reference to the parable in this book called "Parable of the Tar Pit." Look how these parables intertwine with the same information: Here is an enlightened woman who comes into Wo's life and causes Wo to change—and all she has to do is be there!

So it goes that Wo had to know about this unnamed woman's peace and inner joy—and her tolerance toward men. Remember that Wo was now in a state of imbalance and was ill. This was the state necessary for her to surrender enough of her ego to ask another woman about these intangible things. Notice, too, how the parable used one woman to be the messenger for this other woman, even though we are all humans and our gender isn't supposed to make a difference to God. It does when karma is concerned, though, for much of the karma we carry is the energy generated around the opposite sex (father and mother issues, and so on). Lately, science has also discovered that our brains are biologically connected in different ways, and it has finally acknowledged that we actually think differently. (No kidding! I wonder how much money they spent on that? I could have verified it for nothing, had they asked.)

The woman shared her spiritual truth with Wo. The guides were poised and ready for this event. Here was the test they had expected and had waited for. The parable tells us that Wo asked for help alone in her room, and by verbalizing her intent, she started the amazing process that followed. The story goes on to tell of the changes in Wo's life and of the third guide that joined Angenon and Veréhoo down the line. This guide was from a "master Angel-guide group." Again, Kryon speaks of the master guides as being different from the normal ones. To some, this is the same as receiving a higher kind of angel in their lives. All this nomenclature is appropriate, since my translation of Kryon uses only my words. I believe that one could use the words guides *or* angels *interchangeably if desired, and that it really isn't important what you call them as long as you understand the incredible mechanics of why they are here and the love they carry for us.*

So Wo ended up being an enlightened human—forgiving those in her past, recognizing that she was responsible for everything, and finally having real peace. At that point, she was able to partner with a man and make it work—the real test.

Look at what happens next in the parable: Our heroes Angenon and Veréhoo are replaced! What kind of story is this, anyway, where the good guys get knocked out in the middle? This would never work in the movies. How do you think Angenon and Veréhoo felt? Weren't they good enough to stay with Wo from here on? After all, they had endured 47 years of anger and frustration! Hadn't they earned a chance to enjoy the results of the planning they had helped with?

Wo had given intent for enlightenment and was moving toward a status that demanded master guides, and Angenon and Veréhoo knew it and were ecstatic with joy. They departed with much love and no sadness. They had been part of Earth history and celebrated all of it.

Such is the mind of God that one entity can celebrate the joy of the other so completely. Once you truly see the big picture, you can celebrate your neighbor's good fortune and mean it, even if you are feeling that your life isn't going as well as his or hers. Some folks never understand how this can be. Putting on the

"Mantle of the Spirit of God" is what Kryon often invites us to do. This means to carry with us the connection to the higher self, and move into such balance that our first feelings toward all humans are love based, without all the other baggage that used to be dragged in. Honor the one next to you, for his or her process is related to yours, even if you feel it is vastly different.

13
Story of the Two Farmers

AUTHOR'S NOTE:

Most of you are not farmers; in fact, in this country they are becoming scarce! This story is definitely for you, however, and carries a terrific, loving message of Earth changes and the new energy we are seeing take place around us.

There were once two good farmers. Both farmers each owned a crop that they were able to farm on their own, without help from others. But it took all their time, and they worked hard to harvest it. Both farmers were Godly humans, and they honored the land appropriately. This created a fine partnership with the Earth, and they were rewarded with abundant crops each year and were able to provide for themselves and their families. Some of their harvest was used personally, and some was sold at market to provide sustenance and abundance for their families. They lived good lives.

One day an anointed human appeared in each of their fields, claiming to have a message from God. Both farmers were interested and listened intently to the message: The messenger told them that they were dearly loved and that through their hard work they had earned the power to increase their harvest tenfold! It was their gift, and they now had the power within them to do it. In order to activate the new power, all the farmers had to do was to purge the old crop that was growing in their fields. They had to plow it back into the land completely, leaving none of it standing. In addition, they were to search the roots for parasites or fungus and cast out any impurities they found. When they had done so, they were to reseed immediately. In anticipation of their power, the messenger told them that God was changing the seasons, bringing greater sun and rain when appropriate, and shielding them from drought—truly rearranging the components of agriculture as they knew it to allow for their new gift's use. They would still be responsible for accomplishing the hard work of a farmer, but the new gift would eventually make the yield much larger.

Now it was in the time of year that the harvest of the old crop was almost at hand. Both farmers had tall crops that were ready to be cut and sold at market, thereby giving them their sustenance for the entire year to come and to allow them to purchase the seeds for next season's crop. Both farmers were hesitant to destroy their current crop and lose their security for the subsequent season. After all, they thought, what would be the harm in harvesting now, then using the information of the messenger later? The current crop was almost ready, and reseeding at this time would do no good at this time of year, so their thinking went. Any farmer knew that seeds would not grow now.

The first farmer consulted with his family about the message and asked them for advice. After thinking over what he had heard from the messenger, he and his family decided that God would never bring them harm, so it would be best to follow the message "to the letter." Therefore, he destroyed his ripe harvest in the manner specified and totally plowed it back into the land. He examined it for all impurities, casting them out carefully, and then immediately reseeded his fields.

The second farmer did not believe the messenger and prepared to harvest his crop as usual. Shortly thereafter, the rains came. This shocked both farmers greatly, for rain had never come at this time of year before. It watered the seeds of the first farmer's crop and deluged the standing crop of the second. Then came the wind, at a time wind had never blown before. The first farmer's crop was just starting to grow due to the rain, and so the wind could not take hold of it. What was left of the second farmer's waterlogged crop stood heavy and tall and was easily ripped away by the strong winds.

And so it was that the first farmer's crop grew to a quantity and height he had never imagined, and he rejoiced in his new power to create an abundant harvest—just as the messenger had predicted. The second farmer lost his old crop and awaited a time when he could align with the new seasons and again plant his seeds, feeling uncertain and anxious over the new uncharted seasonal changes.

Being Godly men, the first farmer celebrated his abundance by giving of it to the second farmer, and the second farmer, understanding the ways of the Earth, accepted the first farmer's offer without ego or remorse over his decision. Both farmers and their families worked both of their lands until the second farmer again had the chance to plant his seeds in the new season.

AUTHOR'S POSTSCRIPT:

The farmer is used here to clearly represent a human in marriage with the Earth, toiling in harmony with nature to achieve life sustenance. In addition, these farmers, specifically, were independent, able to "farm on their own without help from others." So we have the setup of two humans walking the Earth who depend on the planet for sustenance and who are totally responsible for everything around them. Does this scenario sound familiar? It's a strong metaphor for the way most of us live. The farmers represent those of us walking the Earth right now.

The next part of the setup relates to those of us who live in relative security. Kryon exposes this idea when he states how the farmers led generally happy lives and usually yielded abundant crops each year. This indicates the kind of life most of us have, where we work hard and somehow make it financially from year to year. Kryon also goes on to reveal that the parable takes place in a free economy where "some of their harvest was used personally, and some was sold at market to provide sustenance and abundance for their families." These words are all-important, for they place the story firmly within our free economic society.

THE PARABLES OF KRYON

The greatest revelation, however, are the sentences: "One day an anointed human appeared in each of their fields, claiming to have a message from God. Both farmers were interested and listened intently to the message." This is an amazing clue as to whom Kryon is actually speaking about! What would happen with most folks if a fellow showed up telling them that he had a message from God? Most would throw the guy out and have a good laugh (such is the culture we live in). But these farmers were different because they "were interested and listened intently to the message." Note that they were not just passively interested, but they listened intently. Most of you reading this are seeing where this is going—and what Kryon means is that he is about to give us a parable about two humans living in the new age who are enlightened.

The parable goes on to describe how the messenger lets the farmers know that they have a change coming, but in order to take it, they have to do something different and seemingly illogical. It's something they have not done before, and it goes against what they have been taught works for agriculture.

Look closely at what they were told, and what it means: (1) Purge the old crop—get rid of all your past ways of doing things. (2) Plow it under—bury your past ways so completely that they are truly gone. (3) Cast out the impurities and parasites as you plow it back under—don't keep attachments around, including things in your life that you have always had riding along but that you have intuitively known are wrong for you. (4) Reseed immediately—start growing with the new energy and the new ways of things right now. (5) The messenger then went on to let them know that the Earth around them was going to change, allowing this new arrangement to be comfortable and to support them.

As the story goes, one farmer has a lot of trouble with all of this, since his crop is ready to harvest, and he really doesn't believe everything he was told by the messenger. Kryon tells us that both farmers were hesitant to destroy a full crop, showing *that it was even difficult for the one who finally did as he was advised. This means that what is being asked of us is difficult! It won't be easy for any of us to truly cast out the old ways we do things and embrace the new. Even with vast rewards promised (like a tenfold harvest), it's hard, since we can't really see what is ahead.*

Still, I always wondered as I thought about this parable how a messenger from God could be ignored. Then I chuckled to myself when I remembered that in Sunday school I asked myself the same question when I first learned about Pharaoh hardening his heart time after time, when Moses kept bringing "big-time" proof that it was bad news not to let the slaves go. Was Pharaoh stupid, or what? Now Kryon is showing me the same "hard streak" in us all! It's really difficult to change our ways and habits when they are so dear to us, as we have depended on them for so long.

In the parable, one farmer follows the advice, and the other does not. Shortly thereafter, both are shocked by the Earth changes (rains and winds that had never been seen before at that time of the year). The Earth changes are beneficial to the farmer's crop who had followed the messenger's advice, and indeed his newly seeded crop grows to record heights. The other farmer's crop is destroyed (even though it was healthy and tall when the messenger arrived).

The admonition here is clear: The old ways will no longer work. The Earth changes are going to make them fall as seeds on barren ground, and they will no longer grow. Even the most healthy and successful old energy methods are going to fall away. The ones that will be successful are new, often different, and represent uncharted waters. They are also the methods that will be filled with love, abundance, and positive results.

Finally, the one with the abundance shares it with the one who did not listen! There is no judgment involved and no "finger pointing." The second farmer, who obviously messed up, also does not feel too proud to receive from the one who did well. There is so much lurking in this simple message that it would take volumes to fully describe the wisdom for this new age. Both farmers took responsibility for what they had created, and they worked together in harmony and appropriateness to bring about a "win-win" situation for all.

This parable was intended directly for the enlightened—the teachers and the workers. Amazing validations of the lesson presented here have come forward in many ways, showing that this parable is not to be taken lightly. It actually represents a scenario for the kind of change that is taking place on this planet as you read these words. Take a moment to read it again. It's packed with a wonderful and powerful message.

14
Angela and Her Guide Friends

AUTHOR'S NOTE:

This is one of the first stories that Kryon ever told that exemplifies a life's journey with our angel guides. Originally titled "Angela the Loved," it tells about contracts, guide interaction, and the love of God by women and men in our daily lives.

D ear ones, sitting next to you and bonded to your very essence are entities whom you know as well as you know yourself. These are your guides. Some call them angels or spirit guides, and they are your best friends. They support you in times of joy and fear, and they are assigned to you for life and love you dearly. This is a story about how it all works, presented in truth and love for your learning....

It seems that there were three angels. Together, they were summoned to a great meeting where a plan was taking place to create a planet of free choice. The universe needed a situation where entities would be left alone to seek their own level of vibration so that the universe—the entire universe—would measure the results after a time and know how to proceed. This, therefore, became the mechanics of a wonderful experiment of love, and the word *experiment* is used here only in the highest term of honor.

Angela, being one of the angels, was especially intrigued by the new planet. She heard of the plan and said, "This is truly an honorable event. I would like to be part of it." Both of her friends also decided to participate, and although it took a lot of preparation time in human terms, in Universal time (being in the "now"), all went quickly until the planning session was before them.

So it was that Angela, her friends, and those around who had also decided to participate, became part of this great event. They sat and made great contracts for themselves, for the plan was for each of the three to incarnate into this new planet, and while they were on the planet, their true identity would be COMPLETELY HIDDEN from them. In order to make the tests interact, each one that they would face was to be planned by them collectively. So Angela and her friends spent a great deal of time planning these things. The plans and contracts were complex, for they involved many other entities besides her friends around Angela—all cooperating with the planning—all working on tests for themselves as well. Once the lessons and the tests were set up, it was time for action. Many of the entities within the planning moved into the Earth plane first. Then at the appropriate time, Angela and her two friends moved into the Earth plane together.

Angela had planned with the others that she would come in as a female human. In addition, the plan called for her to have the opportunity for an abusive father, and the father had agreed to play this role with her. Furthermore, Angela was to carry heavy karma, since of the three who decided to come in, Angela had the attribute of a long time-cycle (her Universal attribute), so she would make a perfect human with heavy karma. It was also planned that in her 13th year, there would be an appropriate test for Angela—that is, to lose her mother. Her mother's entity helped with the planning and agreed to have this attribute present itself.

An abusive father and a mother's death were both very heavy attributes for a small human being and were appropriately set in place by the overall plan. It is important to note that no predestination was afoot here. These were challenges for Angela and her human family. Those who would come in and fulfill the heaviest of the challenges around her were doing so by choice and by advance agreement. Each of them would have the option to move into or out of their own plan as they wished once they were part of Earth. Therefore, the windows of opportunity that would create these things were established by agreement. The tests were what the humans would do with each window. Full choice was the option of each human—to go through the plan or not.

So it was that Angela was eventually born into the Earth plane, and the two angels who were her best Universal friends joined her as her Earth Guides—each invisible, but with her in order to hold the balance of the energy while she was biologically alive. They were by her side at every step.

And so Angela was born as a human in September. The plan proceeded on course, and the setups of her karma and the karma of the group around her were in place. Indeed, her father played his planned role, for his karma was to be abusive to her, and so he was, choosing in all his astral wisdom to enable Angela's karmic attributes. This was a trying time for the child Angela. She can remember hiding in a closet, hoping the father would not come home that day, sitting in the dark shaking with fear at what might happen. He did come home, and he stormed through the house in drunken anger until he found her small, dark hiding place—and what followed for Angela was not pleasant and created an energy that stayed with her for her entire life. She remembered what he smelled like, what he sounded like, what fear felt like. Angela had the stamp of an abused child placed on her that night and nights after that time and time again.

Angela got through it, only to find that in her 13th year her mother died. Angela was beside herself, not knowing what to do from that point on. She felt abandoned by all. She removed herself and went to the trees and sat on a stump for a very long time, sobbing with distress at being a child with an adult's burden. Her friends—her angel guides—were with her all the time, giving her energy, holding her hand, shedding tears of their own, loving her through these trials and tests of the human spirit.

She made it through these times, but an interesting thing happened. For the setup was complete as designed, and those who had agreed to supply the play around her had played their roles well, and in the process created new karma for future incarnations that they would all have, too.

What would Angela do with the karmic attribute of the abusive father and a mother who left early? What would it mean to her later in life? Her karmic test was generated, and it was now in place.

Odd as it sounds, when Angela became an adult, the first thing she did was to find a partner who was like her father! The angel friends around her knew why this happened, and they supported her through these times. As it turned out, this partner was also abusive to her.

So as this journey goes, there was a time where the partner eventually left, and Angela found herself abandoned again. Her abusive father had abandoned her in family integrity, her mother had abandoned her in death, and now her partner had abandoned her in love. Angela was at the crossroads of her life! Was she going to turn inward and blame God for her plight? Was she going to "play" the victim from now on? Angela had a choice—the kind that is the flash point of why she came to Earth in the first place. What she did now would make a difference for the entire planet.

In the midst of this test, Angela was prompted to engage in self-examination. Her wisdom that came from having to deal with death and abuse at an early age gave her an overview that helped to balance her reaction to her life's trials. This excited the angel guides around her! They knew that something was going to happen. Indeed, Angela started looking inward to see who she really was, and she started on a spiritual path that would eventually lead to a peaceful life—and the forgiveness of those who had hurt her in so many ways. In the process, her karma was diffused...and Angela raised her vibration, which made a difference for all humans everywhere.

So it was that Angela died in her 83rd year, having completed an incarnation on Earth that was valuable to her and to the whole. Her self-discovery had incrementally raised the vibration of the planet, and she was peaceful with her death.

Dear ones, here is where the story gets good, for after the death experience and the trip to the cave, Angela passed into a great hall of honor. You humans here have never seen anything like this on Earth, nor could you ever remember it from before, for it is blocked from your memory. But I tell you, dear ones, that this is where your colors are given to you each time you finish an incarnation. This is where the honor stripe is given for all the universe to see what you have earned. For wherever you go from this point forward, all Universal entities will recognize where you have been by these stripes. And this planet of free choice that you volunteered for will be remembered and honored for all time. Many will wish to communicate with you for great lengths of time and ask you for stories of what it was like to be part of the grand project called Earth!

Others will stand apart and honor you from a distance—but all will know of your journey—and all will love you for your love and sacrifice. For what happens on Earth affects the entire universe.

This is why God honors you so much! For this, dear ones, is the work that you have chosen to do. And although it may sound grandiose to you, there are tens of millions of entities present for this color ceremony, all in the grand hall at once to celebrate the honor that is bestowed on each of you. For this is a new honor stripe, one that has not existed in the universe before. You who incarnate over and over to this planet are part of a unique set of entities, ones who stood in line for this purpose, and your process fills us (the Kryon) with awe. This is why we sit at your feet. It is why we love you so!

Angela stood before the multitude and accepted her colors, and her angel guides celebrated next to her, and they were honored with other colors as well. It was after the honoring ceremony that Angela was with her friends alone. They began talking together about the marvelous things they had seen while on the planet Earth. Her friends, the guides, began talking to her as they all figuratively held hands, jumped up and down, frolicked, and played against the backdrop of the galaxy of lights.

"Angela, do you remember the time that you were hiding from your father in the closet? Do you remember when we sat beside you and held your hands and hugged you? Do you remember that? We fed you energy to get you through it. We loved you with unconditional love. We held you up when you were too weak to resist. We embraced your heart when you thought it would break with confusion!"

And Angela replied, "Oh, yes, I remember that. Dear friends, thank you for your love. I remember that—yes!"

"Angela," they asked, "do you remember the time your precious mother died, and you sat on the stump out in the forest alone and wondered what life had for you—where you might go and what was to be your future? Do you remember that we sat next to you at that time and held your hands and gave you energy and loved you? Do you remember the extra tears that were ours, and the sharing of the burden? Do you remember that?"

And Angela said, "Ahh, yes, I remember that. YES!"

And her friends asked her, "Angela, do you remember the wonderful times we had celebrating your wedding, and how joyful you were at that time of your youth? Do you remember your glee and your happiness back then? We were holding your hands and hugging you and sending you energy and dancing with you. Do you remember that?"

"Oh, yes, dear friends of mine, I remember," Angela replied. "Wasn't that a grand time?" Then suddenly Angela was still. She spoke with concern. "Through all of these times, my friends, I never acknowledged your presence even one time. I never told you I appreciated you. Somehow I knew you were there. You are my best friends, but I never even said I loved you."

And her friends jumped up and said, "Angela, please remember that you were in the duality of humanism. You were in the anointed space of lesson. You were in the midst of the contracted tests. Do not be reproachful with yourself, for you were and ARE magnificent! The celebration we just experienced honored the journey and the effort. There is no failure in our eyes, only admiration for the journey."

Angela understood the appropriateness of their remarks, and yet there was a stirring within her that caused her to say, "There is something more to be done." With that, and with full agreement of the others around her, she said, "LET'S DO IT AGAIN! Let's go back to Earth! And this time, just maybe this time, I'll see you, and I'll know who you are. And won't that be grand?!"

So we leave the story with Angela returning to the planning sessions with her friends to see if she could again participate in the lessons of humanism, this time making it even better. Such are the mechanics of what keeps all of you coming back and back and back. For the work you do for Earth is a work of love and is of great purpose and importance. When you are not in the chairs you sit in now and not in the bodies you occupy now, you have the balanced mind of God, and you know how honored these things are that we speak of!

Ahh, dear ones, if you could see what Kryon sees, you would see the room filled with those who love you and who are literally bonded to you. Yes, I am speaking to each one of you. And for those of you who believe you have no awareness of these angels or guides, we give you this gift: Later this night when you are alone, dare to ask for those who have been with you all these years to give you a small hug. Allow yourself to feel their emotional presence. For a human being to do this is such an honor to the guides and angels who surround you! You have no idea how they will celebrate your request, and a great fluttering of wings will be felt. When you start acknowledging those whom you have carried with you since birth as your best friends, your lives will begin to change. Believe it.

And so it is!

AUTHOR'S POSTSCRIPT:

*T*here is very little I can add to this story that isn't obvious. Sometimes Kryon gives cryptic parables that need analysis, and sometimes he expounds during the stories to qualify exactly what is being taught. This is one of those parables that contains the focus of our entire work on the planet—and yet the real story here is exemplified by the question, "HAVE YOU HUGGED YOUR ANGELS TODAY?"*

15
David the Indian

AUTHOR'S NOTE:

Here is a story about an Indian who lived on a lovely island with everything he needed—but his curiosity to know more about his surroundings separated him from the rest.

There was an Indian named David who lived on an island. And for those of you who wish to know more about why an Indian was named David, you will have to analyze that later (cosmic laughter). The island that David lived on was a good one and was abundant. David was of the lineage of royalty on the island, for his grandfather was the chief. David lived a fine life on the island; there was an abundance of food, and much grew and could be eaten. David's village and his tribe lived well for many, many years.

Now, the island was surrounded by an odd attribute, for there was a great fog bank that was very thick encasing it, starting three miles from the shore. It surrounded the island completely, and since the fog never came onto the shore, the days on the island were generally sunny and clear. The fog remained offshore at the same distance from year to year like an ominous sign, and no one could ever see beyond it.

David grew up with this fog, and those in the village had experienced it generation after generation. They did not understand it, but they feared it, since every so often there would be a villager who would journey into the fog bank and never return. Even as a boy, David can remember one of the older tribesmen who was near death, who chose to get into his canoe and go into the fog. There were many stories of what would happen if you went into the fog, mostly told at night by the light of the campfires.

The villagers were taught that if anyone ever went into the fog, the rest of the villagers were to go into their houses and their villages and not watch! You see, there was great fear around this evil fog. But David, being royalty, got to watch these few events with the elders as a child, and later as a teenage boy. But the only event he really remembered was the time the old one went into the fog. He remembered that as the old man went into the fog bank, he saw him pick up his paddle as his canoe slid gently into the fog, and as expected, he never came out again. Just as the elders had said, "No one who ventures into the bank ever returns." And those of royal lineage stayed for many hours watching the fog after the old one had disappeared into it, waiting for something that was foretold to happen. For often, after a time they would hear a giant muffled noise, a fearful sound that would strike fear into their hearts, a roaring that they could not understand. David would remember what it sounded like for the rest of his life. Who knows what that could have been? Perhaps a monster on the other side of the fog bank? Perhaps the sound of a giant whirlpool or waterfall, just waiting to claim the lives of those who would go through it?

Now it seems odd that David, in his 34th year, would have made the decision he did, but he felt a pull to the fog! He felt that there was something more to his life that he was missing. Perhaps it was a truth that had been lying dormant for years, and somehow the fog was the answer? It is true, no one had ever come back, but that didn't mean they were gone, thought David. And so David set out with courage, without telling any of the elders or villagers, to see what was on the other side of the fog bank. He got into his canoe slowly and gave ceremony in preparation for what he was about to do. He thanked God for his life and for the revelation of what was to come. He knew that no matter what happened to him, at least he would have knowledge, and that was what drove him on.

And so David paddled silently and gently toward the fog bank. No one was watching, for he did not announce what was taking place. Soon he was on the brink of the fog, and it was coming ever nearer. Then David noticed a strange thing; no one had ever purposely gotten close enough to the bank before to observe anything like this, but it was pulling him into it! The element of fear at this surprising event started to grip him. David did not need his paddle any longer, and so he picked it up and put it into the boat. The canoe disappeared into the fog with him in it. It was still and quiet while David was in the fog bank, as the current kept pulling him forward. It became darker and darker, and then David began to reconsider what he had done. "I am a young man; I have failed my elders, for I was in the royal lineage, and I have chosen a foolish, foolish thing!" David was now afraid, and the fear came over him like a blanket of death, and the blackness started creeping into his brain, and he shook with coldness and emotion as the canoe sped silently along by itself.

David was in the fog bank for hours, and it seemed like it would never end. He cowered in his canoe, for he knew that he had made a mistake. "What if nothing ever changes?" he said to himself. "What if I am here for all eternity and starve in this canoe?" David suddenly had a vision of fear where all those who went before him were now floating endlessly in their canoes, going in circles around the island as skeletons in the dark fog. Would he see the old one from years ago? Would anything ever change? "Oh, where is the truth that I sought?" cried David out loud in the fog.

Then it happened. David came out of the other side of the fog bank! He was astounded at what he saw, for there in front of him was an entire continent: clear, filled with many villagers and villages as far as he could see! He could see smoke coming from their smokestacks and hear them playing on the beaches. There were lookouts stationed along the fog bank who saw him immediately. As he came through, they observed him and sounded their horns in celebration to let the others know on the shore that another brave one had come through the fog. Then David heard a giant roar come forth from the land. A roar of celebration! A roar of honor! They surrounded him with canoes and threw flowers. When he got to the beach, they came and took him and put him on their shoulders and celebrated his coming through the fog. David, the royal one, began a new, enriched life that day.

AUTHOR'S POSTSCRIPT:

*N*ow you might say, *"I know what this parable is about. It's about death, isn't it?"* No, it is not. This parable is about coming into the new energy and even about ascension. It's also about being content within your small group and never venturing out of it due to the "fog" of unfamiliarity. It is about what is before you if you wish to walk the path. For in front of each of you is a fog bank, which sometimes is your fear, and other times is your unchanging nature. Each kind of fog is a different challenge and lesson for each person in varying degrees.

What is it that gives you the most fear? For many of you, it is the fear of succeeding and the fear of being on your contracted path—the fear of abundance! Perhaps it is the fear of enlightenment itself. Maybe it's the fear of change? We encourage you to walk into this fear standing tall. Whatever it is that gives you the most anxiety, that you know is your life's lesson, must be walked into face first with courage, knowing that it is simply a facade. The fear is the fog bank in the parable, and on the other side is celebration. But moving into it sometimes creates a time of darkness—a transitional time to allow you to adjust to what is coming. Those around you will warn you against it, telling you that it is not for you. But part of you knows the truth, and some of you will seek it out for yourself.

Why does Kryon bring you such a parable? It is to exemplify responsibility in this new age of ours. Now is the time of enablement, of responsibility for the entire energy of the planet, and it is the time for you to recognize your path. It's time to look into the eyes of your adversaries and say, "I know you! I know who you are, and I choose to disengage from your energy." This is where the tests are passed and where the vibrations are raised for the planet! For there is no sweeter spot on this planet than for you to recognize who you are. For all of the things that give you grief now can be changed by your intent to make it so.

16
Past Lives, Present Fears

AUTHOR'S NOTE:

This is a set of four stories based on four common fears. It is different from any other set of stories or parables in this book. It was a time when Kryon sat before a crowd in the seaside setting of Del Mar, California. In that crowd were four individuals whom Kryon honored by describing a past-life setting or a past-life experience—sometimes the actual death of the person in a past life was given. The reason was to present us an example of how past-life energy contributes to the karma of this life and helps shape our personal lessons today. The stories are serious and are about real people who were there that evening. Prior to the stories, Kryon gives us a brief synopsis of how karma is carried and why it is there at all. Through all of this, Kryon invites us to see the incredible victory available through realization of the overview of our life's lesson—for that is the secret to passing quickly through these lessons and living a far more peaceful life.

Some of you sit before Kryon and say, "Tell us about fear and faith and anger and courage. Tell us about integrity. Can these things be measured? Do these things have energy?" The answer is YES. You see them daily, and all of them belong to you in whatever degree is appropriate for the karmic imprint that you designed for yourselves when you were not here.

Your karma is your life lesson, and it is carried through a magnetic imprint on one of your hidden strands of DNA. Fantasy, you say? Today's fantasy will become tomorrow's science, and then you may look back at these writings and find hidden wisdom.

Some ask, "You mean a spiritual aspect is carried in a biological package?" Yes. I tell you that your karma, a spiritual aspect, directly involves your biology. Fear creates chemical changes—it makes your heart beat faster and makes your palms sweat. It gives you headaches and makes you faint. Anxiety in a human has been studied by your science as long as there has been human life. The reason behind these seemingly illogical feelings is in the instruction sets from past lives. Your DNA contains many instruction sets that are magnetic. When you are able to break through these basic imprints, this very information will seem less fanciful and far more real. All this information, and the very practical use of it, is literally at your doorstep!

Before you arrived here, you made decisions to go through experiences that create lessons for today. In your current life, you are given opportunities to go through experiences that will void the lessons and graduate you from them. This is what you call *karma* and the resolution of karma. It is the preset sum of all your fears and many of your life's attributes.

And so we wish to tell you about four of your most common fears and the way to walk through them. It is in Love that I come before you to give you this information, and we are going to do it in a unique and interesting way. For I wish to exemplify the four fears by taking you on four small journeys—journeys that exemplify the past lives of four of you seated in this room. None of you will be singled out. If you relate to the past life, feel honored that you have been selected, for God honors you greatly for your service.

These will be the most significant past lives in the room. Be aware that the fears shown here can be caused by any one of a number of things. None of them has to be as dramatic and serious as these. However, these specific ones will show you the kind of humans who are among you and what they have gone through. This is the reason God honors you so much for agreeing to be here to raise the vibration of this planet!

The Fear of Abandonment

We speak to one of you tonight who has a real fear of being left behind—of being abandoned totally. Yet there is nothing in your current life that might have caused such a feeling. I invite you to remember something—something that will create emotion as well as understanding in your heart.

You are nine years old, dear one, a female, just like now. You awaken and find yourself a passenger in a small boat with 14 others. Bobbing up and down on a calm sea, you inhale the salt air and feel the warmth of a rising sun on your face. This serenity is short-lived, however, as your brain races to try and remember why you are here! Slowly you recall, and your heart sinks with grief. Your last vision is that of being roughly carried out on deck in your parents' arms as a ferocious fire rages at their heels. They are almost at a dead run as you are clutched to your father's chest. You can smell the fear on his breath. You remember the sounds of screaming and yelling—the shouts of panic around you. You remember being flung into the air without your father even stopping at the rail. You fall a very long way into the calm ocean. After clearing the water from your eyes, and recovering from the temperature change, your swimming instincts take over and you tread water for a short time until you are lifted into a small boat with the others.

You look backwards at the large wooden ship, now totally engulfed in flames, and your parents are nowhere. They have saved your life, but it was too late to save their own. You look at the others in the small boat, adults each one, and scream at them to do something! You see only the reflected yellow flickering in their faces and eyes as they too are in shock and horror at what they are seeing. They do nothing but watch. Slowly, the great ship slips into the sea as the smoke billows into the sunset, somehow increasing the beauty of the already red-and-yellow sky. There is a great hissing sound as the waters ironically douse the fire that was out of control. Then there is nothing. Swirling bubbles mark the place where a comfortable life of love, anticipation, promise, and caring abruptly came to and end that evening.

It is done. There are no tears. There is a moment, a flash, when you understand intuitively with your nine-year-old Higher Self that this is your contract—that this is the agreement you had with your parents. But the logical order and the spiritual appropriateness escapes you as you feel the incredible emptiness of the abandonment of love. The little girl has suddenly grown up, and the child has seemingly died. For a moment, there is the temptation to join them in the waters—the warm waters of this Baltic sea. But suicide is not in the makeup of children. It only comes later with intellectualization, using the adult brain.

The die is cast for this feeling and this scene to follow you lifetime after lifetime, for it is dramatic, and the lesson it carries must be looked at and realized. And so it is that you live your life with others around you, none of whom will ever show you the love that you received from these special parents. You feel as though you are in a boat of strangers—for the rest of your life.

You know who you are, dear one, in this group, for the attribute of karma that you still have before you is the fear of abandonment. It is not a logical fear in your life, because you have not experienced it here—but you fear it greatly. As a child in this life, you were a problem to your parents because you clung to them and would not let go. Even now you call the remaining one twice a day just to see if she is okay. Relationships come and go because you simply cannot find it within yourself to trust that any partner will remain at your side—and you refuse to go through an unpleasant separation—better to remain alone than that. The flames of the burning ship are imprinted on your DNA like stains on wood, and you live your life moving in and out of them, like weaving a web around a poison strand that can never be touched.

Dear ones, we give you the invitation this night to pass through this karma. You see, there are those of you in this room, and even reading these words, whose lives are controlled by the fear of abandonment. The windows of opportunity come your way to correct this, yet you do not go through them. It would mean taking an action that would stir up the fear, touch the forbidden strand, and you often feel controlled and don't know why. This is the way karma works.

When these situations occur, we invite you to walk straight into them! The tool you now carry is the love of God in the New Energy. This love is all around you. Your guides and angels stand beside you and hold your hands whether you are in the most barren part of Earth or the most populous. Feel this anointed love surround you. Claim it! Cross this painful bridge, feel the love pour into you, and know that abandonment is not in your program any longer. Feel the magnetic code dissipate as you free yourself from this phantom, and know that you are cared for by an energy that will never, ever abandon you. Your efforts will be rewarded with success, for this is the lesson, and the passing of it will raise your vibration and that of the entire planet!

The Fear of Confrontation

There is also one among you who is fearful of any kind of confrontation. This will explain why. You are 32 years old, dear one—a male in this reflected lifetime. You are a female, however, as you sit here in this group.

In this past life, you sit uneasily with others in the chill of night, waiting to stand and emerge in a line of battle. As you move, your armor feels uncomfortable, for you have never had it on before. The helmet, which is forced onto your head, feels foreign and is the wrong size. The shield is heavy, and the sword—you never realized how heavy a battle sword was! You are asked to stand, but you barely can due to the added weight. You are being placed into battle as a last-ditch effort to save your country. It is being overrun by the barbarians, the conquerors, the ones grabbing your land and taking all you own. The small army of your country was overcome weeks ago. Now you are being required by your leaders—in a final effort—to go before this enemy that advances upon you.

Only three days ago, the stewards of government came and gathered you from your fields, for you are a farmer by nature and understand animals, crops, and plants. Now you stand next to those battle-clad with you in the lines who are also farmers, for you all have worked with sheep and goats and livestock. And you stand with the heavy sword in your hand

and realize that you don't know how to handle it, and that you don't begin to have the knowledge of the warrior you are about to face. You are afraid! Your body and brain yell, "RUN THE OTHER WAY!" but you have the silent honor of the love for land and country—and so you sit waiting.

It is time! The sun is rising, and the sounds of the enemy come rolling over the fields with the morning dew. You peek over the trenches, and you see their lines advancing toward you, clanking and thumping with the machinery of war. The battle bell is sounded, indicating that you must rise and move forward. You look at the man next to you, a neighbor for years—one who grew wonderful crops—crops you have tasted many times at events with his marvelous family, and you see the fear and sorrow in his eyes. He avoids your stare lest you see his tears. Both of you simultaneously lift your heavy weapons and armor loads as you stand and advance toward the warriors in your path. There is no thought of fleeing, no thought of saying *no* to your land. The enemy will destroy your farm, anyway, so you might as well die fighting them now.

Oh, the smell of fear is in the air, dear one, as you march toward this noisy line, and you know that death is imminent! There is no turning back. You do not look in the faces of those next to you—those neighbors whom you have known and loved, those whose children you have known by name, for you know you will see their fear, and you wish to give them dignity in their last moments.

As you approach the enemy, the warriors advance quicker. They are anxious to meet you. Somehow they know that their victory is assured. All too soon they are on you! You see the face of the one who is going to make battle with you. He sees you, and instantly he sizes you up. He knows you are a farmer, and he grins, revealing his missing teeth. All seems to be in slow motion as you wonder if he has ever helped birth a calf or tend a flock or raise a crop. Did he have a family, or perhaps nurse a sick animal though a rough time?

He raises his ax high above his head, and you raise your shield instinctively to ward off his blow. With his other hand, he sinks his blade beneath your shield, deep into your flesh. He has tricked you with this basic warrior move, and with a searing pain in your gut you immediately feel your legs weaken under you. It is quick and effective. He knocks you over with his shield and lets out a victory yell. You feel the spittle on your face as he speaks in a tongue you don't understand—and he moves on to his next victim.

You smell the familiar dirt as you lie in the mud listening to the large group retreat towards your farm. In preparation, your family is safe in hiding, and your animals have all been freed. Somehow you are peaceful. It is over. You did all you could, and now it is up to the others. "Good-bye, dear precious family," you hear yourself squawk in a voice that is seemingly not your own. "I will see you all in God's time." It is over, and you know intuitively that you are going home. You feel the warmth of your life's fluid run out of you and spill on the land you love and have cultivated many times. The pain is brief; then there is blackness.

Dear ones in this room, let me tell you—this is why God loves you so much! For events like this create your lessons, and these are the lessons that raise the vibrations of the planet! Is it any wonder that we sit at your feet in awe that you have chosen to do such work?

This painful event from a great past time speaks to you today, many lifetimes later, of your fear of confrontation. It also speaks to you of your hesitancy to join with your government in any venture, for it spelled death to you the last time! Please realize that you do not necessarily have to go through a battle with a toothless titan to have the fear of confrontation. But again, we have exemplified the most dramatic case this night so that all of you will appreciate who is sitting next to you.

We encourage those of you who wish to move through this karmic fear of confrontation to put on the armor of God! The next time con-frontation presents itself in whatever form that creates fear in your body—which makes your heart beat faster, or stirs the chemistry to make you anxious—move directly into it! Feel girded by the mantle of God. This new armor of the Spirit of God is far different than before, because the rules have changed in this new age. This is the age of co-creation with

God—an age where your power is absolute as long as your intent is pure. This is the mantle of love and the sword of truth. There is nothing that can stand against it!

Those on the other side of your new energy confrontation will absolutely be aware of your karmic change as you move into the event— and they will change, too. Watch for it. See how their reactions will not be the same when you put on your spiritual armor and wield your sword of truth. For your actions will push love toward the individual you are confronting—and do more than just confront. It will solve the battle without wounding the warrior...for it will change the one you are dealing with, and it will change you as well!

No matter what kind of confrontational situation is at hand, move into it with confidence and love. Your confrontation is no longer a battle where there is always a loser and a winner, but instead the confrontation itself brings about solutions for both. The mantle of God contains the armor of wisdom, the shield of knowledge, and the sword of truth. Move into it, therefore, with peace and a quiet countenance of assurance. When you do this, your karmic tie will be broken, and you will never again fear this attribute.

The Fear of Unworthiness

Almost all of you have had a lifetime that matches the one given now. Go with me for a moment into this lifetime. If we were to ask you to look down at your feet, you would see in the dim light of the corridor that you are wearing sandals—sandals that you made yourself. There are some of you who cannot even see your feet, for your stomachs are so large due to the fatness stemming from eating the bread that you are making in the monastery! Rumor has it that fasting was invented by the high priests just to keep the friars from exploding. You can be the judge of that.

All of you have had lifetimes in service before God. We can tell you this because there is a commonality among those who are here before me in this group—searching for enlightenment, serious about sitting for an hour or so listening to my spiritual stories. It speaks of who you are and exemplifies your lives.

But, you see, there is something very interesting about this past life. For in service to God the intent was indeed upside down! You have diminished yourselves in service to God—some of you for more than one lifetime. You have groveled as sheep before your doctrine—because you felt that it was your purpose, and because you were told that this was necessary and instructed by God.

Nothing could be further from the truth! Dear ones, you come into this life as enlightened beings with many colors showing with your greatness—showing how important you are in the scheme of things. We have already told you this, and this is why we wash your feet! So it does not serve your magnificence to spend lifetimes groveling in unlit passageways as scribes before a Godhead.

Why did this happen? How could great news of your arrival as honored humans with the image of God, walking in karmic lesson, be translated to such a scenario? Let me give you a hint as to how this could be, how this wonderful message of human honor and empowerment from the great new age master of love could have been twisted so much. Think about this: For hundreds of years, your spiritual leaders were also your governments. They occupied the same seats and passed political and spiritual laws. What is it that men regularly do to create control? I will leave that question for you to answer, for it will show you why governors should never be priests.

This upside-down worship is still rampant within your time now, even though religion is no longer linked to your political leadership. Listen to what your religious leaders tell you today. Does it really sound like the true message of human empowerment as the master of love intended? Modern-day religious leaders will still tell you that you are nothing, born into a world where you cannot win—a world where you have somehow already done some horrible thing that you should be ashamed of. They say you have to put your trust and faith (and your abundance) in a doctrine—then you can be something. This message, dear ones, does not suit your magnificence! This message, dear ones, is NOT accurate information, for you are indeed special when you arrive!

So what karma is produced through lifetimes of monastery service? It produces fear and anxiety toward authority. It creates a feeling of unworthiness, and one where you feel you can do nothing that is good. You feel that only the higher spiritual ones can do anything at all.

When you spend lifetime after lifetime being told you are nothing and that you are sheep, then you are in constant search of the shepherd, and you never feel that *you* are worthy to be the shepherd. Modern-day religious leaders tell you who the shepherd is, and most of them do not agree with each other. Still, they control you. They tell you what to do. They contain your enlightenment. This is wrong! It is a basic fear caused from eons of time spent misunderstanding who humans are! The master himself told you that you are shepherds in training and are equal. Read the words again!

This karma keeps you away from your magnificence. It keeps you from walking through the windows of opportunity because you do not feel worthy of success! You often feel that you cannot do certain things and cannot have abundance while you walk this planet.

Claim your power! God is your partner in this new age, and your intent should be to communicate and discern—not fall on your face and worship to the exclusion of doing the work. Our admonishment is that you pull out the mirror of the Spirit of God and look in it. See who you are. See the brilliant colors that are yours. See the honor that is yours. Revel in it! You are indeed worthy, and the love and instructions of God will support this! God does not wish to control you!

The Fear of Enlightenment and Commitment

The time is more than 4,000 years ago. You, dear one, are female and are in a marvelous procession. The parade started at the palace, and through several hours of winding down narrow streets, you are finally at your destination. Flowers are being thrown upon you, and all are shouting their praise for you. You are dressed in a long white flowing gown, trimmed with elegant gold taken from the mines hundred of miles away. Other women march with you at your side who look similar in their splendor.

Although the crowd is adoring, you do not smile. The protocol is set, and there are ceremonial rules to follow. The procession plods along slowly to the beat of many drums from the musicians marching behind you. There is a large object being carried directly in front of you that leads the parade. It is heavy and has many servants to carry it. The desert air is stifling, and, as normal, there is a hot wind blowing about this time of day. You do not care about the energy you are exerting, for it will make no difference tomorrow. You move ahead, tired but alert. You feel honored, for among women you are a spiritual leader. You and your fellow marching attendants are about to be honored above all the rest and receive rewards far in advance of any others around you.

Slowly, the spectacle winds its way to the designated area where the parade stops. The drums drone on, however, and the musicians move to a place of height as they continue to drum and climb the stairs at the same time. Finally, they turn and face you from their high position, then they stop. Nothing but the wind can be felt or heard. It's very hot. It has taken days to prepare you. Baths and oils and preparation work by the servants of the king have made you a work of art. Your face has never looked like this. It is radiant and colorful. Your hair has many ornaments; gold and precious stones adore your neck and arms. The heaviness of it all is beginning to wear after the many long hours of travel on foot from the palace, but your pride does not let anyone know it.

So here you are, poised at the entrance to the tomb of the Pharaoh. You know what is next. There is a hush while the musicians start the song of the ascension. A plodding rhythm calls for you to walk very slowly. You and the others creep behind the sarcophagus in practiced steps as you descend down the long ramp that will take you into the bowels of the prepared pyramid. More flowers are thrown. Incense is everywhere, and you slowly descend down the ramp toward the sunken entrance. As your troupe marches down the gradual slope, the ramp walls give you some shade and coolness for the first time in many hours.

Suddenly, you are inside. It's actually cool here! There is dampness and some water, and you slowly lose the sound of the crowd from outside. As you negotiate the tunnel, you move into single file—another practiced move. Torches now light the way, and the last thing you hear from the outside is the muffled beating of the slow drums. Reverence is all about you, and the priests lead the way into the final room where you move into the ceremonial circle of eternal life—and wait. You have never been within in the actual pyramid. They never allowed it. All practice was done in the palace within a room that was almost identical to another ceremonial circle—now you know why.

The gilded coffin is set into the great stone chamber, and the lid is lowered. The Pharaoh's mechanics remove the ropes and fulcrums from the stone lid and quickly disappear the way you came in, almost running in their quest to leave. The priest gives the signal, and you take your place in the alcove with the stone seat. Another signal, and you sit. It feels good to sit, but still you do not smile. The priests take their places as well and remain silent.

All is still, then you hear it—a sound that very few have ever heard from your vantage point and that none have ever lived to describe. It is a sound that you know will be one of the last you hear as a human. The afterlife awaits, and the boats have been prepared not too far from you. There have been years of preparation, yet there is something happening within you—FEAR! Are the others feeling it? You are going to die now! This is real!

The sound goes on for a very long time. Distant as well as close-up rumblings of lids descending, doors being slid shut, stone after stone being lowered in place with hydraulics that only work one way. Once the sand is gone from the tubes, the stones are down—there's no way to raise them. No thieves will ever be able to penetrate the stone vault. The Pharaoh's mechanics on the outside begin their work to erase the tunnels and build new ones to confuse any who would rob your precious chamber of its king. You know that long before the workers are finished sealing the tomb, you will be dead.

The torches are slowly going out, and you realize that soon it will be pitch black. This is the last light your eyes will ever see! The air is becoming stale. You have never been afraid of being in confined places, but this is different. It's your coffin! Still you sit, but now you are shaking. You hear around you mild whimpers and sobbing, and you realize that you are not alone in your horror and fear. It was all fine and good to be within the spiritual entourage of the Pharaoh, but you really didn't expect this day to ever come. You thought he would grow much older before he died; instead his death came so soon! You knew that those around him would go with him to his grave, including you, but it was all such a fantasy—something in the future. You committed yourself to a spiritual quest and stood as a leader in the Pharaoh's court for years. Now you are almost in the dark in a small room that will never have air or see the sun again. You fight the panic of it all. YOU CAN'T GET OUT! IT'S GETTING HARD TO BREATHE! IT'S DARK!

As if knowing what you are thinking, a priest gets up. You barely see him working in the dimming light. He kneels and takes leaves out of his pouch and mashes them together on the stone floor. The light is almost gone. He takes the remaining smoldering torch and lights the leaves. You see more light as the leaves catch fire in their small pile on the floor. Briefly, you catch a glimpse of the others in their alcoves; some are wide-eyed and filled with terror. You smell a sweet fragrance, and you know what it is. How humane, you think. No one told us of this. Thank you, dear sacred one, you send thoughts to the priest as you sense a feeling of escape. You breathe deeply of the smoke of the leaves, and you feel light-headed. A few more deep breaths and you lose consciousness. There is no more anxiety. The drug has put you to sleep so that you may pass from life into death without caring. Finally, there is a smile on your face—and that's the way the thieves will find you when they finally cut through the stone to steal the treasures from your arms and neck—the ones that your king selected to take into eternity with him.

Dear ones, you have just witnessed the death of the entire attendant group around a great Pharaoh, for this was the way of things. When the Pharaoh died, his spiritual attendants went with him to the tomb so that he would have the same aides around him when he went into his afterlife. There is one of you here in this group who fears commitment and enlightenment so greatly that you will literally run the other way before you decide to seek God again. You are uncomfortable right now, and you remember that to get close to any spiritual intent is to die! "Never let it happen again," shouts your innermost being. Your karma is set. Spiritual commitment equals death!

It's time for you to change. Again, the love of God will temper your fear. It's time for you to metaphorically re-enter the tomb, for this time there will be no closure of it. This time you may pass through it to continue living on Earth. God asks you to consider giving intent for full enlightenment this very moment. Join the group of attendants around the King of Kings, but this time, live a grand life of your own while on the planet. No horrible premature death will take place if you decide to do this, and your karma will be broken! Listen to the voice of love as it speaks to you now, and know that these feelings never have to visit you again. Never again fear the spiritual path, for hiding in the phantom of your karmic fear is the energy of home!

And so it is!

AUTHOR'S POSTSCRIPT:

*T*hese *stories were especially potent for the attendees that night. There was great silence in the room after Kryon finished. The faces of those listening to these words showed that some of them related to the scenarios even though they were not the actual people being highlighted by Kryon. So many of us have walked through similar situations in past lives that these stories tend to re-awaken some dim and distant feelings, and for a moment, the part of us that is God and knows all things resounds with the truth of who we really are and what we have been through. Some of us incarnate in groups, and therefore many of those listening that night may have actually been there and experienced the same events in other ways. In Kryon's words, it is again said, "With all this, is it really any wonder that God loves you so?"*

17
John the Healer

AUTHOR'S NOTE:

Here is a story that has the potential to relate to many of you reading these words, for it is understood that those interested in this book may also be facilitators and healers. Not only does it expose many of the things that are happening with healers right now, but this parable also gives the "golden rule" of healing. Do you know what it is?

John the healer was a spiritual man. He had a wonderful practice, and he understood his science well. Many came to John and were healed; however, there were always a few who were not. But John was starting to feel uncomfortable; for you see, the new energy was upon him, and he knew the new age was here. John was uncomfortable for a number of reasons. The chief one was the fact that his healing practice was not as successful in his eyes as it had been. In other words, he was not at peace. He was having fewer and fewer healings on his table, and it made John question whether he should be a healer at all!

John would meditate often, for he was a powerful meditator. It guided his life, and he understood prayerful communication with God and listened intently to what God said in return. This had always worked before, and he knew it would work again. We're going to let you in on the conversation between John, his guides, and his higher self. This will be enlightening for you and important for the story.

As soon as John sat down, his angel guides said, "Oh, John, hello! How are you?" (They were very familiar and friendly guides—as all are.) John ignored the activity and began his breathing ceremony (not hearing them). Moments later, John was ready, so he was prepared. His head and feet were in the right position. He was facing north. His hands were upright. "Oh, God," John began, and his guides interrupted, "Hello, John, we love you!"

John said, "I need help. Nothing is working," and he named the humans who had come to his healing table by name. He asked, "What about this one? I have been working on his back for so long, but nothing is happening!" He implored, "I pray for help here. Heal this person. Make this happen...give me this...do these things." He hardly knew what to ask for, there were so many requests.

And his angel guides replied, "Oh, John, WE LOVE YOU DEARLY! All of the power that you need is here, and we stand ready for you." Then they gave him such an incredible wash of love that he knew he was in the presence of God.

John felt he had answers, and he believed that things were going to change. But the next time he saw the human with the back trouble, he realized that it had gotten worse. John did everything that he knew how to do, yet there was no healing. Back he went into his meditation with the same results. He would sit for a long time until he felt he was in the right position, and God would be there, and he would feel the love of his angel guides and of his higher self. They would say, "Oh, John, indeed we love you. You are so powerful."

And John would beg God, "Oh, please, show me what to do in my healing room." And so life went on for John in this way.

Now, John had a sister. It was almost adding insult to injury that his sister was also troubled with ill health and that he seemed unable to do anything about it. So he sat with her and he prayed, and he sent her energy. He used his science, the things that he knew worked, but his sister did not get better. She seemed so troubled all of the time.

Finally, after a great amount of time, John had reached his limit. In anger, he stormed into his meditation area, sat down on the couch, and exclaimed, "I've had it! Where are you?"

"Hi, John, how are you?" His angels immediately answered him. John was so shocked that he almost fell off his meditation pillow.

"How can you be here so quickly? I'm not ready."

"We've always been here, John," his guides replied. "We're with you even in the healing room."

"You told me I was powerful," John said. "You gave me incredible answers. I felt them in the love that you sent. Yet nothing is happening! I'm at my wit's end. What can I do?"

John's guides faced him and said, "Oh, John, we're so glad you came. Listen—it doesn't matter how good the stove is; the food will never be cooked until the burners are hot."

Now, John was not a fool, and he asked them, "The burners—they're me?"

"Yes," replied the loving angel guides.

"What can I do?" John asked.

"What is it that you choose to do?"

"I want to be in my contract!" stated John loudly.

Oh, the fluttering that went on when he said that! For that's all they had to hear. This time John didn't specify whose back was to be healed. He didn't specify what he specifically needed or where the power should come from or on which day he should feel better. John finally said, "I want healing for myself. I want to be in my contract. I want my passion to be fulfilled. I want to do what I came here for."

Through his angels, God said to him, "John, it took so long for you to ask that. You shall have it! It is yours, even as you ask."

When John arose that night from his meditation, he realized that things had changed, for he had a new peace. Even before he went back to the healing room, he knew things would be different. God had told him that all he had to do was to take care of himself, and everything else would be added. When John walked into the healing room, amazing things started to happen, for he was given further knowledge. "I'm going to lay my hands here today," he would say to himself. "It's different. No one told me to, but I know it's going to be the right thing to do." Results were immediate. John knew that God was standing over his shoulder, winking at him, saying, "Oh, yes, that's right. Now try this." John was beginning to have results like he had never seen before! He told the ones who came to him to get ready to be healed. He had ceremony with them prior to ever touching them. They thought he was crazy—until they were healed. Then even more people started coming to him—John the powerful healer.

And so it was that John went to see his sister. John literally danced into her room, all aglow, knowing that her healing was next. He saw her light up! No more scowls, and yet he hadn't even touched her.

"John, what has happened?" she asked him. "I've been so worried about you!" Everything stopped. Then John realized that his own torment had spilled over into the very ones he was trying to treat. Time after time he had come into her room and dragged his own anxiety with him. He had actually hindered her health by his own worry. No wonder nothing worked!

"God told me you're going to be healed," John warmly announced. Then he had ceremony with his sister, and he felt the peace of God overwhelm them both. He shed tears of joy in his newfound knowledge and thanked God for such a cooperative effort that brought such wonderful results. His sister was indeed healed because she was ready, and because John had taken care of himself first—and his power and wisdom had increased greatly. John's intent had changed not only his own life, but all those he touched from then on.

AUTHOR'S POSTSCRIPT:

"*W*hat is the key to becoming a powerful healer?" is a question asked by many. Know the science of your craft, then balance YOURSELF! Call for your contract to be fulfilled. This balance creates additional knowledge, better tools, and vastly increased wisdom to use in the new energy. All of these wonderful healing gifts are yours, but they cannot be implemented until you take care of yourself first. When you meditate alone, it is not necessary to beg for the healing of your clients. Save that for group meditation, when you gather with others to send positive energy to those around you and the planet as a whole. Your knowledge is the basis of your healing, and your intent is your power. What you do in personal meditation should be for YOU. Your contract as a healer is what creates the actual power to clear the way for curing others. The more it is fulfilled, the stronger you will be as the healer. Co-create the total marriage to your contract, and watch what happens!*

18
Five Karmic Lessons

AUTHOR'S NOTE:

When you were young, did you ever absolutely feel that you were born to do something? Perhaps you watched a craft being performed or smelled something familiar in some strange place that created a "déjà vu" experience? Maybe you even pursued it to no avail? If all of us have past lives, it is only logical that there might be strong remembrances carried over that don't necessarily play an important part in this lifetime—but they are still present as remembrances at the cellular level.

I know that some of you who knew what you were going to do when you were five years old then went on to successfully do it! What's the difference? This is a story about five people who had strong karmic feelings carried over from other lives. It shows us what they did with them (or didn't do with them), and how it affected their lives. Things are not always what they seem, and within each story Kryon will comment on what happened.

Mary the Barren

We will talk now about Mary the Barren. Now when Mary was a very small child, she knew intuitively that she was born to be a mother. When other little girls her age played with dolls, they played with one doll, but Mary played with six. Mary knew all about children. She knew what made them happy and how to bring them up. She was wise in this area, you see, since Mary had been a mother before. Lifetime after lifetime after lifetime, Mary had raised children. Sometimes as many as eleven were hers. Mary was born to be a mother!

As she proceeded along her life, Mary found a partner, a male human who said, "I want a big family."

Mary said to herself, "This is the one for me." Together they made plans, and they obtained a very large house in preparation for many children. But unfortunately, as life unfolded itself, Mary had no children, for, to her shock, she was discovered to be barren, and all of the knowledge that she had regarding children seemed to be for nothing. She was distressed and distraught. She was angry at God, and she wondered how such a trick could be played on her—to come into this planet with such a knowledge of children and then to be denied! Her mate? He did not last a year. For, you see, he wanted his own biological children, as Mary did. He wanted to look at their hands and their fingers and know that they were just like his, and that his biology was their biology. Mary was left alone.

Mary got over her anger at God, for she was spiritually aware and she knew it. A window of opportunity had come for her to learn more about the feelings she had inside. It did not make sense to her that God would trick her so greatly, so she sought out answers in the company of others who brought her information; she discovered herself.

The main thing that Mary did immediately that made all the difference was to take responsibility for the events in her life. She understood through studying that she had indeed planned what had happened. She did not understand why, and she still cried in the middle of the night for the lost children that she was not to have, but she took responsibility for the situation. It wasn't long afterwards that Mary had a vision, and then she knew what her mission was. For the vision showed other mothers throughout the world reading her words and her wisdom. You see, Mary was supposed to publish information about the raising of human children, and so she did. And by the time Mary passed over again to the cave of creation and on to the hall of celebration, she had written seven books in all. They went planetary. Tens of thousands of mothers benefited from

Mary's work, her insights, and her experience. In retrospect, standing on the other side, Mary understood what had happened. Oh, yes, she had come in with the knowledge, the "residue" of her many past lives, but she had misinterpreted it. She was not to have children, for that would have gotten in the way of her true mission! It took accepting responsibility for who she was and the problems that she experienced, for her to turn around and see what to do with her knowledge.

Hold this in your mind, for there are others for us to tell you about.

John the Abundant

Let us speak of John the Abundant. Each one of you knows this John. He was born unto this planet with the ability to create wealth. Everything John touched made him wealthy, and it was indeed his karma for it to be so. Many looked at him and said, "He must have been a fine person in a past life to have this positive karma." But they did not understand at all what his lesson was. Even as a boy, John was collecting money from other children for this and for that—a service here, an act there. By the time he was out of school, where others were just starting, John was already on his way to abundance. It went on from there, for he collected and amassed a fortune.

So much wealth did John have that he did not have the ability as an individual to spend it all in his lifetime. Even so, John occupied all of his time creating more, and he became unhappy. Then he became angry. For John did not have a clear vision of his mission. It was too easy to create abundance, so John became an irritable and complaining person. There were those who did not ever want to be with him, he was so angry! So the only ones who were with him were the ones who he paid well to be— which was their own karma. And so John died an unhappy man. It was only after he was on the other side that he realized what his lesson had been. He had selected one of the most difficult lessons of all, one that he was unable to work through.

Dear ones, there is scripture that speaks of this, and we wish to tell you what it means and what it does not mean. For the words are translated to say that, "It will be almost impossible for a wealthy man to see the gates of heaven." Let me tell you what this means. It is this: It is extremely difficult for anyone with great abundance to become enlightened, and that statement stands alone without anything around it. This was John's lesson. Could he come down onto the planet, experience this kind of attribute, and still find enlightenment? For the windows of opportunity that he had to find enlightenment had passed him quickly, and he had not glanced to the left or to the right. The pursuit of his abundance occupied him totally.

Now, some have taken this scripture and extrapolated an entire scenario of poorly thought-out rules around the subject of abundance. "What God really meant," they say, "was that you cannot be wealthy and have enlightenment! And," as this faulty logic continues, "if you have wealth, therefore you are not enlightened. Furthermore," as the final stage of this thinking goes, "to find God, you are to give all of your wealth away" (usually to some organization ready to receive it with the purpose of helping you get rid of this spiritual burden). "Only then will you have enlightenment." These same individuals (it gets worse) have actually equated being poor with being enlightened.

Believe me, dear ones, this is not the case. We ask you to see the common sense of it. We have told you before that we wish you to have abundance. In other stories, we have taken you on journeys where you opened the door to your inner spiritual-life rooms, and one of them is always filled from floor to ceiling with beautiful things—gold and wealth (see "Wo and the Rooms of Lesson" in this book). Now, why would we show you these things, invite you to co-create your own reality, then give you a postulate that says you cannot be enlightened and have abundance? The reason is this: You *can* be totally enlightened and have wealth beyond measure.

The difficult part of this attribute is simply that one who is born into the planet with the ability to create abundance easily has extremely heavy karma. Will he or will he not turn and look at his spiritual side and become enlightened? In other words, the distraction for the creation of power is almost insurmountable. That is the extent of it. All of you are invited into abundance, each and every one. The scripture is simply a statement of difficulty and an admonition to be aware of it. To have enlightenment and earthly wealth requires great balance and a true sublimation of ego. These attributes don't exist together very often. When they do, you know you have met a very old soul. Blessed indeed is the one who knows God and has abundance!

Philippe the Fisherman

We wish to talk to you about Philippe the Fisherman. Now, Philippe was not on this continent, but this is indeed a real story of a real human being. All Philippe wanted to do from the time he was a child was to fish. For you see, Philippe carried into his lifetime a karmic residue of many, many fisherman lifetimes. He was a fisherman over and over, interacting with groups of fishermen around him, and he knew it. For when he was a child, all he wanted to do was go to the seashore and mingle with the adult fishermen. He learned to tie all of the knots, and he was excellent at it. He intuitively knew about the seasons for fishing. He intuitively knew what to do and when to do it to harvest a large batch of fish.

Philippe's father was a man of means and also a man of legal training. He did not want Philippe to be a fisherman, for unknown to either of them, his father had an agreement on the other side with Philippe, and it was all part of his father's karma to fulfill this mission. The father was disturbed that Philippe wanted only to be a fisherman, for he had greater plans for him than that.

And so he removed Philippe from the seashore—far inland where Philippe was enrolled in schools of legal learning. So it was that Philippe became a legal expert, and he excelled in it. In fact, as he grew, he loved it. Indeed, he thought about the life of the fisherman, but instead he turned the fishing experience into a hobby. He would go to the seashore anytime he could to sail a vessel that he had purchased with his own money. There he would get to smell like a fisherman for a day or two and revel in the experience.

As the life of Philippe continued, he was invited into the leadership court of his country, and again Philippe excelled. For you see, he had integrity. He had spent time with fishermen! He had an affinity with nature and the creatures of nature and of Earth itself. Philippe carried his wise ways into his work, and he became a great leader in his country, rising to the top leadership position. The people of his land loved him. Somehow Philippe reminded them of a common fisherman, and they responded to such a personality.

So, you understand that the past-life residue that Philippe carried may very well have kept him at the seashore as a fisherman had it not been for his father. For his father's mission was to raise Philippe to be a wise leader, and he had done so. Philippe's mission was to use the attributes of the fisherman and apply it to the government of his people. Together Philippe and his father had an anointed plan; it was called "karma," and both humans had walked through it perfectly. The result was that many were helped, and the planet's vibration was changed.

Elizabeth the Royal

Let me tell you about Elizabeth the Royal. You see, when Elizabeth was born, even as a baby she held her head high. Most of you know that this is unusual. A child has weak muscles and cannot hold his or her head up. But Elizabeth held her own. Oh, indeed, Elizabeth was royalty, and she knew it. The only problem, dear ones, was that Elizabeth's parents were not royalty.

Elizabeth was born into a poor group; gradually, through the years, this angered her, for she knew she was special. She was a princess on her way to being a queen, but nothing around her visibly agreed with that feeling. And so she irritated the other children with her countenance, and later on she irritated the other adults as well, for she wanted things a certain way. She carried the air of being royal in a poor family. And very much like the first story we gave you of Mary the Barren, Elizabeth's opportunity came to fruition. A woman friend took her aside one day and explained to her the workings of God. And Elizabeth, looking at her own life, said, "I firmly take responsibility for the way I feel—born as a princess without the royal family. So what is my mission?" she asked. Then she acknowledged, "Maybe it is not necessary for me to have had a royal family for me to be royal."

So Elizabeth, on her own, decided she would create her own position. And everything she tried worked! The windows of opportunity flew open for Elizabeth as she moved through the leadership of her group and co-created her own reality. And in her 43rd year, Elizabeth found herself respected and admired by all. Because of her talents and who she was, she had indeed created her own royalty. So once again the past-life residue had served her, but not in the way that she thought it might. The alchemy is clear in this story. For Elizabeth had taken a potentially disappointing situation, and through understanding and enlightenment, turned it into an appropriate one of honor. Elizabeth the Royal...was indeed Royal.

Now, dear ones, from these four stories, you might ask the question, "How can I tell the difference between a past-life residue and a contract or a mission? For they look the same." Mary the Barren thought she was going to be a mother, John absolutely knew that he was born to be abundant, Philippe the Fisherman thought he was born to fish, and Elizabeth thought she should have been a queen!

It is very easy to know the difference, and here are important attributes. All of the planning sessions of karma, the ones that are happening at this moment for you, are based around windows of opportunity that are action items for you individually. That is to say, they are planned in love for your enlightenment, and they face you squarely at potent times. Some windows are planted there to show you what you are not supposed to do. On the other hand, activities that you try that work well for you are obviously your missions. We invite you, if you do not know the difference between a cellular intuitive feeling and a mission, to walk directly into the challenge of finding out. Some of you have felt that you should be this or should be that. Perhaps you should go here or go there, but you're uncertain. Many of you will have to venture out in order to find out the difference between a past-life residue and a karmic contract or mission, for there is often a blurry line between the two.

It is this blurry line that karmically invites you to venture out to find the difference. Do not be afraid of wasting time or resources on something that seems to have failed, for it may have given you truth! It is this very action or intent of the venturing out that signals God and your angel guides that you have decided to move into what you planned! Do you see the irony of all of this? If you sit in a heap and worry and fear what you are supposed to do, then nothing will happen. It is only when you go beyond your fear and step into action to find out, that the "engine" of your lesson is engaged. Sometimes your action seems to result in failure, but the truth is that you have indeed found out if the feeling is residue or mission. It is the human who keeps trying the residue over and over who is the foolish one. It will simply never work.

So if Philippe had tried to be a fisherman, it would not have worked for him. There is something Philippe never found out that was hiding in his biology. He would have been sick constantly if he had proceeded with his plans to make fishing his life's work. This is another way God honored him to help him find his mission. It would not have worked for him; and if it had not been for his father, he would have had a chance to look at this clearly. Instead, Philippe was successful in moving into his mission quickly because of another human at his side who had come in for that very purpose. Do you see how important humans around you might very well accelerate your mission?

There is no judgment by God of whether you pass through your karma or not as you reach the other side, having seemingly failed a life's test. As was the case of John the Abundant, there was no judgment at all, not even by John. Instead, John received a hero's welcome in the hall of honor just like the others. It is in the incarnation that the honor goes. There is never a time when God judges whether or not the lesson was accomplished. The honor is in walking the road, not in which direction was walked.

David the Loved

I wish to tell you now about one who comes into the Earth with no karma, but only a mission. And we wish to tell you now about David the Loved. Now, David was born with part of his brain missing. He was an intelligent child. He had all the facilities of consciousness, but the parts that were missing were the parts that controlled his growth. And so it was that the doctors knew that David would not live very long, for there was no way that he could do so with the parts missing. David's entire purpose for being was a mission. Although it was not obvious yet, it would become so. David had young parents who loved him dearly, and he surrounded himself with others who also loved him dearly.

So it was that David had an amazing life for the few years he was on the planet. There were those who took him places that a young person would never have seen. He was showered with love and given every opportunity for learning. And yet so it was in his 12th year that he passed over. For David's mission on this planet was to give a gift to his parents.

Oh, if you told his parents that it was a gift, they would have been insulted! There was never a worse time in their lives due to the sorrow of his passing. It would not have helped the hurt of their hearts to know of David's mission. Just like it is with you, dear ones, when you know someone is passing over, it does not help at that moment to know that it is appropriate. For when the moment occurs, the hurt is there, and at that moment no amount of spiritual wisdom will replace the welling up of emotion. The hurt of the heart is the greatest wound any human will ever face.

David, that precious little one, was sorely missed. And so it was that his parents mourned him, as is appropriate with these things. But you see, David had an agreement with those parents, and his young parents had an agreement with David. David's passing presented a window of opportunity, even when they were at their lowest ebb, for the two young parents to discover a path of quickened enlightenment, a step that they took in their search for peace that they never would have taken except for David's gift. And so it was that both of those parents lived great, enlightened lives and became healers, administering to many over the years. The sorrow was transmuted to joy and healing. And so it was that their enlightenment was complete, and their karma was fulfilled because of the gift of David the Loved. What a waste it would have been if David's parents had never seen the gift and had instead wallowed in their sorrow and let it consume their lives.

David's entire mission was to allow for the enlightenment and healing of hundreds of humans in a future that David was never to be in. His love was in his gift to his young parents, and their love was their ability to see his gift and look for what it meant. So the seeming sacrifice of the one created joy for the many. The spiritual beauty of this story is that David is eternal, and the 12 years he spent giving his gift was a only a blip on the time line of a much larger event—the elevation of the planet Earth.

AUTHOR'S POSTSCRIPT:

*A*ll I wanted to do as a child was to be in the service. My ex-wife, Jan, will verify, even to this day, that when I see uniformed men and women, I feel like I should be with them. I was placed in a military school when I was eight and spent three years there alone as a boarder. I knew what it was like to be in the service, and yet I was never a part of it. When I went on the bridge of a ship in San Diego, I recognized the chair I used to sit in, and I knew I was all Navy. I felt I had my purpose, went though Army ROTC in high school, and made plans for NROTC in later college years in order to have a career as a Naval officer. But this was a past-life residue, you see, and the things that God did to keep me out of the Navy were amazing!*

The first thing was that I had allergies. I got called during college for Vietnam to go up for a physical, and they failed me. They said, "You can't be in the service because you have allergies." Now I know why God gave me allergies. Then it was later that I found out that I get seasick! (Can you see the great Navy officer leaning over the rail in the midst of battle? This is a cosmic joke!) Then at the age of 50, I found out that I was born with one kidney! I could never have passed a complete physical for NROTC. There is simply no way I would have made it in the service of this country, and yet that's all I wanted to do!

I had lifetime after lifetime of military service. It was natural, and I sought it out again when I came in this time. Being born into my karmic group in the Navy town of San Diego was a real challenge for a guy who had a karmic Navy residue, but a spiritual mission—then to be placed in military school when I was eight!

So God put blocks in my way to show me the difference between a past-life residue and a contract. I waited until I was in my late forties before I found my mission, always wondering if I should have been a Naval officer. And the human one that I have the agreement with is here next to me (speaking of Lee's wife, Jan Tober). She was the placeholder for me and got me to where I am—just like Philippe's father did. So now perhaps some of you have a better understanding of Jan's participation in the Kryon work, which I talked about in other publications. It was profound. It's a karmic contract. It's a mission, and I'm glad God honored me with the blocks that kept me from following a false path, and with the partner to show me the right one.

19
Aaron and the Globe of Essence

AUTHOR'S NOTE:

Here is a short story given by Kryon before an audience in Sedona, Arizona, about a man's search for youth, healing, and wisdom. Money was no object as he traveled the world looking for his elusive dream.

Dear ones, Kryon gives you these parables and these stories on purpose, for they are metaphoric and usually do not always represent an actual person on Earth. These parables and these stories are given to you in love—oh, such great love. For they have to do with human self-awareness, and they have to do with healing and long potential lives.

Aaron was on the Earth as a wealthy man, and when he was in his 40th year, he was disturbed by what he saw in the mirror. What he saw there was a man who was beginning to change and age. He didn't like what his face or his stature was turning into. All around him he saw his friends catching various diseases, and some of them were even dying. So he said to himself, "What can I do that would change this? Surely there must be an answer. I know I have my wealth for some reason."

Now, Aaron was a Godly man with a great lineage. He thought, I will use my wealth to discover what some have called the fountain of youth. And so he went to a very wise man and asked him, "Does the fountain of youth exist?"

The shaman said to him, "Not exactly, but there is something we know of as the "Globe of Essence." It is real and it is physical; it will extend your life and will heal your diseases. It will also give you great wisdom."

"Oh, wise man," Aaron said, "tell me, where can I find this Globe of Essence?"

"Well," replied the wise one, "one of the ways is to find the chalice of Christ—"

"Oh, no!" Aaron interrupted. "That is the Holy Grail, and I do not believe in that. My religion does not support these things."

The wise man smiled and said, "Aaron, believe it or not, the Globe of Essence, the Chalice of Christ, and the Holy Grail were all carried within the Ark of the Covenant."

Aaron thought, How can this be? The Ark was considerably before Christ. Aaron ignored this last statement from the shaman, pursuing only what he heard that interested him.

"Tell me, where should I look to find this Globe of Essence?"

The shaman replied, "It is for you to have if you choose, for we can see your contract clearly, and we know that you could be the one to find it. All you have to do is begin your search and trust God to lead the way."

Aaron was very excited, for he interpreted this to mean that he was the one scheduled to find the Globe of Essence for the planet! Once it was discovered, Aaron thought, think of those he could help and heal—for he would have a long life, as well as those around him...his friends, his relatives. Oh, this was even better than he had thought. He believed the wise man, for there was no reason not to.

So Aaron began his search, thinking, Where shall I go first? Answering his own question intuitively, he said, "I will go first to those spots on the planet that I know have the highest energy." So he went to Sedona (audience laughter). He searched all around, and he spoke to the guardians of the canyons. The guardians said, "You will not find it in the canyon. You must look in other places." So his trip took him to some of the most sacred places on the planet.

"Where is the highest religious place?" Aaron asked himself. Again answering himself, he said, "It is my home! I will go there." So Aaron went to the Holy land and sat in front of many religious leaders, some of whom had never heard of the Globe of Essence, and some of whom said, "Yes, we have heard and we know. Continue your search; indeed, you are one who may find it."

So Aaron went into the other areas, the areas of Egypt that were close by. He asked the same questions and got much the same result. He went to the land of Peru and to the land of India. He sat in front of some who said they personally *were* the Globe of Essence—that all he had to do was to remain with them and give them his attention and his possessions. Aaron knew better, for he knew that it was an object, something that he could touch, and that it was for all humanity and not for just one group.

Now, this search of Aaron's took him many, many years; he was growing older the entire time, and he was changing. This was frightening him, and so Aaron started to worry. The worry interrupted his body's function, and Aaron became sick.

Aaron was on his death bed surrounded by those who loved him. He knew he had not found the Globe of Essence, and those around him did, too. He was angry at the wise man who told him he would find it. "What kind of trick is this?" he asked. "What has God done to me?" Aaron was ill, and depressed by the fact that the Globe of Essence had escaped him so completely. His family had watched his quest consume him, and they told him to stop the search for his own sake. He was very tired and longed to sleep.

The next morning he awoke, and this time he stood up. He felt wonderful, but something was different. As his guides came closer to him, he realized that he had indeed passed over. Aaron was not happy at this moment, and he said to his guides as soon as they were before him, "I know who you are, and I know where I am going. What foolish trick is this that I have not found the promised Globe of Essence, for I was told by the Holy man that I would. Have you all deceived me?"

His guides smiled at him, and in perfect love they embraced him with their energy. They asked him to turn around and look behind him. There in the place where Aaron had lain was the Globe of Essence! There it was! It was physical, and he could touch it. It had weight and substance, and it had been in his heart the whole time! Aaron was dumbfounded at the implications of what he was seeing.

He looked around the table at his relatives, and he was shocked. For among those living humans that were sobbing and mourning his passing—in each one was a Globe of Essence as well!

Then Aaron understood that there was not just one Globe of Essence. "It was for all humanity," the wise man had said. "You will find it if you search." But the wise man never said there was only one! And then Aaron knew. And he looked at his guides, and he understood.

He smiled and said, "Thank you. For now I understand my contract and my lesson." Then he turned and walked between his angel friends toward the light—a place he had been many times before. He was not interested in remaining a moment longer in what seemed to be a low vibrational energy.

Even in his short time in the new vibration, Aaron understood that all things learned during his lifetime would be passed on to his next incarnation, and he could hardly wait. For he knew of the trip through the tunnel—through the cave where the record is kept of his incarnations. And then on to the hall of honor, and after that the planning sessions and the return to the planet. For when he returned, he knew that he indeed would be the one to find the Globe of Essence. He would do it as a child, and he would live a very long life. For he would remember this time; he'd remember the lesson that the Globe of Essence is the gift of the precious part of God within each Human.

AUTHOR'S POSTSCRIPT:

*T*his parable is not lost on any of you. Kryon says that there are those of you who sit reading these words by appointment! God gives you the ability to reach out and discover the elusive Holy Grail, for this is the Globe of Essence which is GOD IN YOU. It is the part of God that resides in each of us, which many call the "higher self." Here is a story that shouts, "Reach out and take it and be healthy. Live a long time. Be in your sweet spot. God wants you to remain and live very long lives."

Some of you are saying, "This cannot be, because I look around me and I do not see God residing in the troubled humans around me." Kryon says that when enough of us find our Globe of Essence, we indeed will look around us and see the changes. But it must start in the room you are in right now, and rooms like this all over the planet. In your quietness, you may search for what you carry from birth, and through your personal discovery, you may change the way things work around you, which will have an effect on others and which can eventually change the area you live in! You carry with you the seeds of the Universal Spirit of God and all the healing and wisdom that goes with it. God invites you to reach inward and discover the reality of this and the peace that comes with it—and the planet will change because of what you do in your most quiet time.

20
Wo and the Big Wind

AUTHOR'S NOTE:

God has promised us that being "in our contract" means being in our passion. It also means that we will be in the right place at the right time for everything that we have planned for ourselves in this lifetime. Here is our last story—one that might make you think twice about what you feel is "the right place at the right time."

We have spoken before of the individual entity whom we call Wo. Now, Wo is a name we give to this human walking on the planet. Wo isn't meant to represent a male or a female, for when you are not here, you are neither. But for the purpose of this story, and to make it easy to tell, Wo will be a male. For this is the story and the journey of Wo and the Big Wind.

Wo was an enlightened individual and lived on a very small island with many others. Wo lived a good life, for he was indeed on a spiritual path. We would call Wo a warrior of the light, for Wo meditated and followed God. He had fine children whom he taught the essence of God through his love. Wo was greatly loved by his neighbors, for they recognized that he was a good man. And so we find Wo living on the island, and daily Wo would say, "Oh, God, I love you. I want so much to be in my contract—the right place at the right time. That's what I want."

As Wo moved forward in his life, year after year, he would daily go down to the beach, and with the sound of the surf crashing in his ears, he would get as close to the water as he could without getting wet, and there he would sit. Wo would say, "Oh, God, put me right where I belong. I don't care if it takes me away from here. I want to be in my sweet spot—my contract."

Now, you see, Wo was doing this correctly, and he was greatly honored for this. Wo would also say, "And in this new age, oh, dear God, there is something I would really like as a gift. I know there are some who never get this, but if it's appropriate, let me see my angel guides—even just once." So now you know the inner workings of Wo's life and his mind. This is who Wo was.

A great storm approached this island that had tremendous ferocity. Wo was frightened, for it appeared as though the storm was going to pass right through his home. In hundreds of years there had never been a storm like this one, for it was powerful indeed. As it approached, there were many who left the island. But Wo remained, knowing full well that he would be in the right place at the right time, just as he had co-created. Any minute Wo expected the wind tomiraculously change course. But you see, it didn't. Instead, it got worse and worse. And so residents were sequestered in their homes and told, "Do not go out. You will be harmed if you do."

So the folks stayed in their houses, and they watched the winds come and the waters rise. They saw their homes start to disintegrate, and pieces of other homes fly by. They were very afraid. But Wo was silent. He did not talk to God about what was happening. You see, Wo was angry. In fact, he was mad, for Wo felt that he had been betrayed.

"How many years do I ask for one thing, and now when the time arrives, I don't receive it?" complained Wo, as the winds grew stronger and Wo grew angrier. "God did not deliver my family and me from this inappropriate place!" yelled Wo in desperation as he heard and felt the back porch of his home tear from its attachments. Then the power failed. Wo heard the trucks coming through the street to pick up the people. The speakers on the trucks announced, "You're not safe. Get in these trucks while you still can. We're going to take you to the school where the building is solid. There you will have a safe shelter."

And so it was that the large trucks went about gathering all the people of the island, taking them to the various schools and churches. Wo ended up in one of the largest schools that was near his home. He and his family braced themselves for the short trip from the truck into the school, and with many other neighbors, struggled against the wind and driving rain to the entrance. Once there, he looked into his neighbors' wet faces— all blank and fearful, but in Wo's eyes there was only anger at God that he should find himself in such a situation. Everyone made their way down the stairways to the basement of the great building. As they crouched in cold corners where they thought it was safe, indeed the power failed there, too—and they were in the dark. Out came the candles, but then the water started coming in, and the winds started tearing at the very fiber of the school building itself. They started hearing the groaning of the cement and of the wood. They huddled in the dark, terrified, making no sounds of their own at all.

Then Wo came to an astonishing conclusion. He realized that he was not afraid! He was very angry, but he was not afraid. He looked around and saw those huddled down the hallways in ankle-deep rising water, freezing without any heat or even candlelight, since the candles only lasted for an hour. He also saw their terror. For, many that night felt that the entire group was going to die. How could it not be so, for they were told that the eye of the storm was not even upon them and that they were going to experience winds that were even worse. If the school disintegrated, they would surely be at the mercy of these elements of wind and rain. No human that night had ever experienced the power of nature like they were experiencing now.

And so Wo stood from the place where he had been seated in anger. He hugged his family and said, "There's work here. You will be safe." And he looked into the eyes of his children, and he said, "Look, there is no fear in my eyes because I have been promised that we are going to be safe." Then Wo left and began going from neighbor to neighbor and from group to group. Wo told them of his love for God, and he told them that God had never failed him. He told them that they would be safe, and he imparted to them the love that can only come from an enlightened human being! As he left each group, he saw that the terror also left, and like a black cloud had dissipated, they were left with hope. Some of the groups started singing songs, so instead of terror and the silence of fear, the sound of singing replaced it. Some of the groups started laughing by telling humorous stories of their lives, and their fear diminished. The terror left.

Wo, as he made his way from group to group, did his work that night. And like some kind of miracle, the fiercest winds never arrived. Instead, the storm reversed itself and went on its way, slowly diminishing instead of intensifying. So just about the time Wo's work was done, the storm had abated enough that the people got the word to return to their homes in the very trucks that had brought them to the school. The sun was coming out, and Wo realized that they had been there all night. As they walked outside, the wind had almost totally died down. How quickly it retreated! The birds were singing and the sun came out, and everyone made their way back to their homes. Oh, and some of them had great sorrow that their homes were destroyed. And, oh yes, Wo was among all of his neighbors seeing that his roof and porch were gone, and the water had come in and ruined many things.

So it was in the weeks that followed that the rebuilding began, and it went smoothly. Slowly on the island, a story began unfolding. You see, there were news reports of what had happened that night in the school. People were telling stories of that fearful night, saying, "There was a man and his associates who came to us in the dark at the worst moments of our fear. They told us that we were safe, and they gave us hope. They replaced the darkness with love and peacefulness. They brought sanctuary to our terrified consciousness, and they also brought humor. They gave us song, and it changed us that night, for we were no longer afraid. Our children responded first, for we saw in the eyes of the children the fact that they were no longer terrified, and then we relaxed. The man's name was Wo."

Group after group reported this amazing event, and to Wo's embarrassment, they asked him to come to a ceremony where he would be honored. And so, begrudgingly, Wo went to the ceremony and heard the testimony of the neighbors telling how he and his associates had helped that night.

After the ceremony, Wo went to the beach, where he sat down next to the water. Then Wo realized what "being in the right place at the right time" meant. He realized that all of his prayers and all of his co-creative ability as a human being in the new age had come to fruition. You see, Wo had prayed to be in the right place at the right time, and that's exactly where he was! He realized that his prayers had been answered 100 percent. Then Wo wept, for he realized that 100 percent co-creation meant that his guides had also been seen that night. Every group of neighbors had seen three: Wo and his "two associates." Wo knew that he had gone into the darkness alone to help his neighbors that stormy evening in the school—so he thought! Yet everyone had seen his angels. God had answered his prayers—all of them.

So, although Wo was not aware of it at the time, his angelic guides had been seen clearly in the candlelight. His neighbors had described them, and through the voices of those he helped, Wo saw his angels! Oh, it's true that he had lost his home, and it's true that some possessions had been destroyed, but the contract that he had agreed to before he came had been accomplished, and everything paled in comparison to that. All of the co-creative prayers had centered around being in the right place at the right time. Wo realized that God had honored him with a complete, full miracle of co-creation.

From that time forward, Wo knew what it meant to co-create and pray for his contract. He knew that it did not mean that he would be spared all of the tests. It did not mean that he would not be present when the Earth shook. It meant that he would be in his sweet spot, and he would be in total peace when these things took place. And it meant that he would be available for facilitation of other human beings when it was needed the most. It changed his life, for he discovered his passion—that of being able to bring peace to the lives of others, in the right place at the right time.

AUTHOR'S POSTSCRIPT:

*W*hen I agreed to do the Kryon work, I expected that I would be directly in my contract. I expected my "sweet spot" of passion to allow me to be "in the right place at the right time," for all of the things to be perfect and appropriate. That is what God promised. In my innocence of the way that spiritual things work, I didn't understand that being in my sweet spot required the dark tests that came with it.

I loved the fact that tens of thousands of new age people all over the planet appreciated the books and wrote to tell me so. This, indeed, was a sweet spot! I was astounded to receive an invitation to the S.E.A.T. group within the United Nations and to actually go there and speak...and to meet such wonderful planetary light-workers. I was amazed when the Kryon magazine took off, and thousands subscribed—and when my America On-Line folder became the most popular new age venue in their history.

Then came the attacks on the work, and like Wo I became angry. "How can I carry around a white paint can for years and suddenly some call it black? How can one light worker attack another? Where is the love?" I couldn't understand why the name of Kryon was being seen by some as evil and treacherous. The misquotes, the twisted words—"Why would someone do such a thing?"

Now, in retrospect, I see that God put the integrity of the work right in the fire! It caused people to rethink what was being offered. It made discernment a key issue in this new age. It made us all think twice about believing just any message that happened to come from any entity.

Through all the rethinking, Kryon emerged as the love-filled messenger that he said he was, and thousands throughout the country reaffirmed it in writing and in verbal thanks. I had gone through my "big wind" and had sat on the beach with Wo and also wept with the joy of knowing that I was exactly where I was supposed to be.

Afterword

Stories are magnificent ways to communicate messages of life! The 20 you have read in this small book exemplify two years of Kryon story-telling in front of large groups all over the planet. Kryon is a messenger of great love and wants you to know personally that it is no accident that you are reading these words. There was something here for you—did you find it?

in Love...
LEE CARROLL

About the Author

Lee Carroll is the author of the KRYON book series, a love-filled suite of works that speak of the good news for planet Earth. Found in metaphysical stores all over the planet, the books have become a source for renewed hope as we move into the uncertainty of the next milennium. Website: **www.Kryon.com**

We hope you enjoyed this Hay House book.
If you would like to receive a free catalog featuring additional
Hay House books and products, or if you would like information about the
Hay Foundation, please contact:

Hay House, Inc.
P.O. Box 5100
Carlsbad, CA 92018-5100
(760) 431-7695 or **(800) 654-5126**
(760) 431-6948 (fax) or **(800) 650-5115 (fax)**
www.hayhouse.com

⸺•⸱•⸺

Published and distributed in Australia by:
Hay House Australia Pty. Ltd. • 18/36 Ralph St. • Alexandria NSW 2015 •
Phone: 612-9669-4299 • *Fax:* 612-9669-4144 • www.hayhouse.com.au

Published and distributed in the United Kingdom by:
Hay House UK, Ltd. • Unit 62, Canalot Studios •
222 Kensal Rd., London W10 5BN • *Phone:* 44-20-8962-1230 •
Fax: 44-20-8962-1239 • www.hayhouse.co.uk

Published and distributed in the Republic of South Africa by:
Hay House SA (Pty), Ltd., P.O. Box 990, Witkoppen 2068 •
Phone/Fax: 2711-7012233 • orders@psdprom.co.za

Distributed in Canada by:
Raincoast • 9050 Shaughnessy St., Vancouver, B.C. V6P 6E5 •
Phone: (604) 323-7100 • *Fax:* (604) 323-2600

⸺•⸱•⸺

Sign up via the Hay House USA Website to receive the Hay House online
newsletter and stay informed about what's going on with your favorite authors.
You'll receive bimonthly announcements about: Discounts and Offers,
Special Events, Product Highlights, Free Excerpts, Giveaways, and more!
www.hayhouse.com